ISBN 978-1-397-36799-0
PIBN 11377387

1 MONTH OF
FREE
READING

at

www.ForgottenBooks.com

By purchasing this book you are eligible for one month membership to ForgottenBooks.com, giving you unlimited access to our entire collection of over 1,000,000 titles via our web site and mobile apps.

To claim your free month visit:

www.forgottenbooks.com/free1377387

English
Français
Deutsche
Italiano
Español
Português

www.forgottenbooks.com

Mythology Photography **Fiction**
Fishing Christianity **Art** Cooking
Essays Buddhism Freemasonry
Medicine **Biology** Music **Ancient
Egypt** Evolution Carpentry Physics
Dance Geology **Mathematics** Fitness
Shakespeare **Folklore** Yoga Marketing
Confidence Immortality Biographies
Poetry **Psychology** Witchcraft
Electronics Chemistry History **Law**
Accounting **Philosophy** Anthropology
Alchemy Drama Quantum Mechanics
Atheism Sexual Health **Ancient History**
Entrepreneurship Languages Sport
Paleontology Needlework Islam
Metaphysics Investment Archaeology
Parenting Statistics Criminology
Motivational

PROCEEDINGS

OF THE

SUPREME COUNCIL

—: OF :—

SOVEREIGN GRAND INSPECTORS GENERAL OF THE THIRTY-
THIRD AND LAST DEGREE

ANCIENT AND ACCEPTED

SCOTTISH RITE

FOR THE

DOMINION OF CANADA.

—————

——···⤞SPECIAL SESSION,⤝···——

HELD AT THE CITY OF HAMILTON, TWENTIETH DAY OF
MARCH, A. D. 1879,

—: AND :—

——···⤞ANNUAL SESSION,⤝···——

AT THE SEE OF THE SUP∴ COUNCIL, MONTREAL,

EIGHTH DAY OF OCTOBER, A.D. 1879.

THOS. DOUGLAS HARINGTON, 33°, Prescott, Ont.

M∴ P∴ Sov∴ Gr∴ Commander.

JOHN WALTER MURTON, 33°, Hamilton, Ont.

Secretary General H∴ E∴.

HAMILTON:

TIMES PRINTING COMPANY, 3 HUGHSON STREET.

1879.

PROCEEDINGS

OF THE

⋇∻SUPREME⸹COUNCIL⸹OF⸹THE⸹33°∻⋇

OF THE

ANCIENT AND ACCEPTED SCOTTISH RITE OF FREEMASONRY,

FOR THE

DOMINION OF CANADA.

SPECIAL SESSION, 1879.

In accordance with a resolution passed at the last Annual Session, and by the authority of the M∴ P∴ Sov∴ Grand Commander, THE SUPREME COUNCIL OF THE 33RD AND LAST DEGREE OF FREEMASONRY, for the Dominion of Canada, held a Special Session, in the hall of the Rite in the City of Hamilton, Province of Ontario, on Thursday, the 20th day of March, V∴ E∴ 1879, corresponding with the 24th day of the Hebrew month *Adar*, 5639.

PRESENT:

Ill.·. Bro.·. THOMAS DOUGLAS HARINGTON.
Sov.·. Gr.·. Commander.

  "   "   HUGH ALEXANDER MACKAY,
As Lieut.·. Gr.·. Commander.

  "   "   JOHN WALTER MURTON,
Secretary General H.·. E.·.

  "   "   HUGH MURRAY,
As Gr.·. Master of Ceremonies.

  "   "   WILLIAM REID,
Gr.·. Captain of the Guard.

The Supreme Council opened in full at half-past two o'clock P. M.

Letters of excuse were read from the following members of the Supreme Council, viz :—

Ill.·. Bro.·. ROBERT MARSHALL,
Lieut.·. Gr.·. Commander.

  "   "   JOHN V. ELLIS,
Grand Chancellor.

  "   "   DAVID R. MUNRO,
Grand Master of Ceremonies.

  "   "   WILLIAM H. HUTTON,
Grand Marshal.

  "   "   COL. W. J. B. MACLEOD MOORE,
  "   "   EUGENE M. COPELAND,
  "   "   ROBERT T. CLINCH,
  "   "   JAMES DOMVILLE,

which were accepted as satisfactory.

The M.·. P.·. Sov.·. Gr.·. Commander read the summons announcing that this Session was called for the special purpose of ballotting for the Illustrious Brother WILLIAM BENJAMIN SIMPSON, 32°, member of Montreal Consistory, to receive the 33°, and for any other business that should come before it.

Ill.˙. Bro.˙. W. H. HUTTON, Deputy for the Province of Quebec, having nominated Ill.˙. Bro.˙. SIMPSON at the Last Annual Session, the vote was taken and the Ill.˙. Bro.˙. SIMPSON declared to be duly elected.

Ill.˙. Bro.˙. WILLIAM REID, Grand Captain of the Guard, presented his credentials from the Supreme Council of Colon as their Representative near this Council, and was received and welcomed.

A courteous and fraternal letter from Ill.˙. Bro.˙. F. RAMUZ, our Representative near the Supreme Council of Switzerland, was read, announcing the receipt of his credentials from this Supreme Council, and expressing his satisfaction thereat.

A letter from the Supreme Council of Egypt was read, requesting the exchange of Representatives, etc., and was ordered to be held over, to be presented at the next Annual Session in October.

A circular from the Supreme Council of Italy was presented, and ordered to be transmitted to the Grand Chancellor for his Committee on Foreign Correspondence to report upon.

The Sovereign Grand Commander gave notice that he would at the next Session move that the Supreme Council of Egypt be recognized. He also announced that the subject of simplifying the titles of the degrees and officers of certain Bodies of the Rite would be considered at the next Annual Session.

Ill.˙. Bro.˙. BRENTON D. BABCOCK, 33° of the Northern Jurisdiction, U. S. A., was announced, received and heartily welcomed.

Ill.˙. Bro.˙. WILLIAM BENJAMIN SIMPSON, 32° being in waiting was then introduced and had conferred upon him, in full, the 33rd or last degree, and was duly invested and proclaimed as a Sov∴ Grand Inspector General, and an active member of this Council.

The labours of this Special Session being over, the box of fraternal assistance was passed, and the amount collected handed to the Commander in Chief of Moore Consistory toward the benevolent fund of that Body.

The chain of union was then formed and the Supreme Council was closed in due form at half-past 4 o'clock p. m.

T. DOUGLAS HARINGTON, 33°,
Sov∴ Gr∴ Commander.

JNO. W. MURTON, 33°,
Sec∴ Gen∴ H∴ E∴

PROCEEDINGS

OF THE

❖SUPREME COUNCIL OF THE 33°❖

OF THE

ANCIENT AND ACCEPTED SCOTTISH RITE OF FREEMASONRY,

, FOR THE

DOMINION OF CANADA.

ANNUAL SESSION 1879.

The Supreme Council of the 33° of the Ancient and Accepted Scottish Rite of Freemasonry, for the Dominion of Canada, assembled in Annual Session, in the Hall of the Rite, at its See in the City of Montreal, Province of Quebec, on Wednesday, the 21st day of the Hebrew month *Tisri*, 5640, corresponding with the eighth day of October, A. D 1879.

PRESENT :

Illustrious Brother THOMAS DOUGLAS HARINGTON,
Sovereign Grand Commander.

" WILLIAM HENRY HUTTON,
As Lieut∴ Gr∴ Commander.

" JOHN WALTER MURTON,
Secretary General H∴ E∴

" HUGH ALEXANDER MACKAY,
Treasurer General H∴ E∴

" JOHN VALENTINE ELLIS,
Grand Chancellor.

Illustrious Brother DAVID RANSOM MUNRO,
> *Grand Master of Ceremonies.*

" ISAAC HENRY STEARNS,
> *Grand Standard Bearer.*

" WILLIAM BENJAMIN SIMPSON,
" COL. W. J. B. MACLEOD MOORE.

The Supreme Council was opened at 12 o'clock noon.

The roll being called, the following members were declared absent :—

Illustrious Brother ROBERT MARSHALL,
> *Lieut.·. Gr.·. Commander.*

" BENJAMIN L. PÉTERS,
" HUGH WILLIAMS CHISHOLM,
" JAMES DOMVILLE,
" ROBERT THOMSON CLINCH,
" EUGENE MORTIMER COPELAND,
" HUGH MURRAY.
" WILLIAM REID,
" JAMES KIRKPATRICK KERR.

Letters explaining the cause of their absence were read from the following :—Ill.·. Bros.·. MARSHALL, CHISHOLM, PETERS, CLINCH, MURRAY and COPELAND, and verbal excuses were presented by various members of the Council for Ill.·. Bros.·. W. REID and JAMES DOMVILLE ; whereupon the following resolution was carried,—"That whereas the Ill.·. Brothers MARSHALL, MURRAY, PETERS, REID and COPELAND have hitherto been regular in attendance at the sessions of this Council, the excuses just presented on their behalf for their non-attendance at this session be accepted as satisfactory."

Letters were received from the following Illustrious members of the Supreme Council of the Northern Jurisdiction

U. S. acknowledging invitations to this session, and in the case of two stating their inability to attend, viz :—

Ill∴ Bro∴ VINCENT L. HULBURT, 33°, Illinois.
   "   "   GEORGE O. TYLER, 33°, Vermont.
   "   "   ALBERT P. MORIARTY, 33°, New York.

It was moved by Ill∴ Bro∴ ELLIS, seconded by Ill∴ Bro∴ MUNRO,—"That the proceedings of this Council, at its Annual Session, October, 1878, having been printed and distributed, the same be now confirmed."—Carried.

The proceedings of a Special Session of this Council, held in Hamilton, on 20th March of the present year, were read and on motion confirmed.

Ill∴ Bro∴ W. B. SIMPSON, created a member of the 33° at the Special Session above mentioned, was duly welcomed.

The Sovereign Grand Commander then delivered his Annual Address, as follows :—

ADDRESS

To the Supreme Council, 33°, of the A∴ & A∴ Scottish Rite of the Dominion of Canada, and the Officers and Members thereof, GREETING:

ILLUSTRIOUS BRETHREN,—

If we look back, it seems but a brief period since we last assembled together, in Annual Session, and I had the pleasure and privilege of addressing you. Our "Chain of Union" still happily remains intact, and not a link has been broken since we then exchanged thoughts and opinions, and took brotherly counsel together. Thanks be to God for his many mercies.

The past year has been a peaceful and harmonious one, as far as our Rite is concerned. I know of no cause of complaint against the several Bodies and individual members acknowledging our obedience. Their loyalty and allegiance have been true and trusty.

I need not unnecessarily occupy your time by attempting to particularize the condition of the Rite, inasmuch as the reports of your Illustrious Deputies for their respective Districts will do that better than I can, and the same may be said in relation to Statistics and your Financial affairs, which our Grand Treasurer and Secretary General will explain. To each and all of these Officers I tender my thanks for their kind assistance during the past year. They make my work a labor of love.

Our Relations with Sister Supreme Councils remain most satisfactory. The able President of the Committee on Foreign Correspondence will doubtless present you with another of his interesting Reports on this head,—reports which we receive and study with so much pleasure. Such Proceedings as have come to us from those Illustrious Bodies will be laid before you by our Secretary General, or Chancellor.

On the 20th March last, I held, by request, a Special Session of the Supreme Council at the City of Hamilton, on which occasion the Degree of S∴ G∴ I∴ G∴, 33°, was conferred upon Brother WILLIAM B. SIMPSON, 32°, of Montreal, a very worthy Freemason and one of high standing in the antient craft, and I felt a personal gratification in introducing him to membership in this Supreme Council, having for a long time known and esteemed him.

We were disappointed at not meeting our Illustrious Brethren from the Maritime Provinces, who were expected, but were prevented at the last minute from being present. Brother HUTTON was also absent to our regret, the mortal illness of a friend being the sad cause. Ill∴ Bro∴ BABCOCK, 33°, of Cleveland, Ohio, U. S. A., was good enough to favor us with his company and assistance.

When at Hamilton I had the satisfaction of witnessing the working of the 15°, 18° and 30° of our Rite, and I bear my willing testimony to the very beautiful exemplification of those several Degrees, and to the praise due to the several Bodies of the Rite in that city.

Notices of motion were given at that Special Session as follows, viz :—For the simplification of Titles in the various Degrees, &c.; and, for the recognition of the Supreme Council of Egypt, &c.

The Hamilton Brethren extended their hospitality to us, and a very enjoyable evening was passed at a truly sociable Banquet.

I have granted only three Dispensations during the past year. One for the special conferring of the 32° on Brother EDWARD MITCHELL, 31°, of Hamilton ; another to confer the 15°, 16°, 17° and 18° on Brother SAMUEL W. RAY, 14°, of Prince Arthur's Landing, waiving the statutory time between them, and the third to confer the 31° and 32°, waiving the statutory time between them, on Brother THE REVD. ST. GEORGE CAULFIELD, 30°,—these Dispensations being granted for special good reasons assigned, and borne testimony to by our Secretary General.

I received a very kind and brotherly invitation from the Supreme Council of the Northern Jurisdiction, U. S. A., to attend its Annual Session in the City of Philadelphia, on the 16th September last. It was with unfeigned regret that I had to excuse myself, for reasons that I made known to the Ill∴ Grand Secretary General. I would have indeed much liked to have met my Brethren, on that very important and interesting occasion.

I have been favored by Ill∴ Brother ALBERT PIKE, 33°, the Sov∴ Gr∴ Commander of the Supreme Council of the Southern Jurisdiction, of the U. S. A.

with several valued communications. 1st, I have received from him a new Book valuable to the Rite, entitled "The Book of the Words." Like all works emanating from him it is most erudite, and the copy sent is a gift to this Supreme Council, which I have handed to the Secretary General for presentation to you, and for which our thanks are due. 2nd, I am in receipt likewise of the proceedings simplifying the Titles of Degrees, Bodies and Officers of the Rite, as decreed in March last to be the Titles hereafter to be used exclusively in the Southern Jurisdiction of the U. S. The Supreme Council of Ireland has, I understand, decided on the same line of action, and I think the Supreme Council of the Northern Jurisdiction of the U. S. has expressed an intention of examining into the subject. This matter has been mentioned to you before, (see proceedings 1878, page 16,) I strongly advise its consideration. The existing Titles of the Rite are cumbersome and behind the spirit of the age, and in addressing one another, what can be more pleasing than to make use of the simple Title of " Brother !"—I leave the matter to your wisdom. 3rd, Ill.·. Brother PIKE has sent to me his Proposed Articles for a Concilier League of Supreme Councils of the 33°, including a " Declaration of Principles," a necessary and fundamental one, being a belief in the existence of a true and living God, and also a proposed " Confession of Faith," to be required of all persons seeking to receive the 32°. I need only submit this Document to you, free from remarks, to receive at your hands the deliberation such an important matter is justified in expecting. The League is formed at present by the Supreme Councils following, viz :

1. The Southern Jurisdiction of the U. S. of America.
2. Ireland.
3. Scotland.
4. Central America.
5. Greece.

I cannot refrain, however, from referring you to Art. 3, Sect. 6, page 5, which enacts—" That no person can ever be recognized as lawfully invested with any " Degree of the Antient and Accepted Scottish Rite, by having received it, or a " Degree so numbered, or claiming to be such, as a part of the *Rite of Mizraim*, " or of the *Rite of Memphis*, or in a Body of either, or from any one conferring the " Degrees of either."

Even if you should decide not to become at present a component part of the above-named proposed League, our Statutes and Regulations may properly be amended by the introduction of just such an article as I have quoted.

Our Ill.·. Friend and Brother PIKE has kindly advised me that he received a communication from certain Masons in Ontario, impugning the legality of this Supreme Council under the Constitution of 1786, and suggesting to our Brother PIKE the necessity of all our Proceedings being pronounced invalid—of our Warrant being declared void, and that this Dominion of Canada, as far as the A.·. and A.·. Scottish Rite is concerned, belongs really to the Supreme Council of the Southern Jurisdiction of the U. S. of America, and should be possessed by that Body, and that we should rightly acknowledge allegiance thereto.

Our Ill.·. Brother PIKE has sent me copies of his share of the correspondence in reply, (one of which is attached hereto, see Appendix A,) which like all emanating from him, is courteous in the extreme. I need hardly say he settles our constitutional legality and standing as a Supreme Council.

The singularity of the proceeding is, that the very Brother who organized our Body, with the known assent of every existing Supreme Council, and whose name is a household word in the annals of the Rite, should be asked to undo his own work, and stultify his own deeds!

With several Supreme Councils we have not as yet exchanged recognition, viz: Spain (see Proceedings 1878, page 20), Chili, Central America, Argentine Republic, St. Domingo (see Proceedings of 1878, page 17), and Hungary, all of which appear to be acknowledged by the Supreme Councils of the Southern and Northern Jurisdictions of the U. S., except Spain and St. Domingo. I have not the Records of other Councils.

From New Grenada I have no further communication to report. As regards Egypt, I suppose recognition thereof need not be postponed (see Proceedings of 1878, page 76), and with respect to Mexico I have not yet acted upon your recommendation for fraternal relations, by an exchange of Representatives, because I have not felt satisfied with the action of that Supreme Council in expelling Brethren desirous of establishing the first three Degrees of the Rite as an independent Body. I concur fully in the remarks of your Committee on Foreign Correspondence, from which I quote (see Proceedings 1878, pages 16 and 17),—" It would be wise for all Supreme Councils to abandon control over "the Symbolic Degrees. This would promote harmony, whilst it would not "interfere with good government. We do not read with any satisfaction notices "of the excommunication of Masons because they have sought to establish "a Masonry of Three Degrees." Many Councils have done this, surrendering such Degrees to Grand Lodges as representative Bodies, and the present Symbolic Masonic generation cannot do without such a system. Where no Grand Lodge exists the Rite may be admitted to be perfectly legitimized in governing for the time those Degrees. I would like you to give this matter further consideration. It is true that some Grand Lodges hesitate as to recognizing and entering into friendly relations with Supreme Councils, 33°, but there is no small amount of inconsistency in this, when it is borne in mind that a large proportion of Brethren of the Craft are really holders of the A.·. & A.·. Scottish Rite Symbolic Degrees, and that from Grand Masters downwards they rank as undisguised members thereof. Credentials presented by representatives from Foreign Supreme Bodies of the 33°, are neither questioned nor objected to that I can discover, which is surely another form only of recognition. If Grand Lodges were to cut off all but Grand Lodge made members of the Symbolic or Craft Degrees of Freemasonry, it is probable that they would find themselves in connection only with some half of the Freemasons of the Globe.

The Royal Arch Degree is acknowledged (Ancient Craft Masonry being defined in England as consisting of three Degrees, including the Holy Royal

Arch), although it is historically shown to be derived from the Royal Arch of the A∴ & A∴ Scottish Rite, or what is now the same thing, from the old Rite of Perfection of Twenty-five Degrees, and yet cordiality is not extended towards the Body that gave birth to the Royal Arch itself.

I must apologize for occupying your time and attention so long, but I think t well to submit everything that crosses my mind connected with the Rite. I will only put on record a few more remarks. You will be glad to know that the misunderstandings, alluded to in my address of 1878, as existing between some of our Toronto members have been cleared up, and it is reported to me by our Ill∴ Deputy for Ontario that complete harmony was early re-established, and all' s progressing well at Toronto. Our Deputy reports likewise that he has received applications from Winnipeg, Guelph and Ottawa for the establishment of Lodges of Perfection there. I hope to be able to say at our next Annual Session that they are at work. Winnipeg is some distance off but the facilities for reaching it are fast increasing, and we have a very zealous Deputy.

Death has of course been busy during the past year, and Brethren have been called to their " rest." Our sorrow is due for their departure and our earnest sympathy belongs to their surviving relatives and friends. The decease of at least one of our own members is made known to me, that of Ill∴ Brother ARCHIBALD MACALLUM, M. A., 31°, of Hamilton, who, it is said, being a life long teacher, was well able to judge of the value of the Masonic lessons he received, and impart them to others. He is spoken of as one worthy of high regard.

And now I will conclude by expressing a hope that we all may be spared to meet again at our next year's Annual Session. I, for one, have reached the allotted three score years and ten. May we each and all work for the prosperity of our Order as becomes our rank ; may we each and all be prepared to meet the last and inevitable summons ; and may our God bless and save us all. So mote it be. Amen.

T. DOUGLAS HARINGTON, 33°,

Sov∴ Gr∴ Com∴ &c.

MONTREAL, 8th October, 1879.

After the reading of this address, it was moved by Ill∴ Bro∴ H. A. MACKAY, seconded by Ill∴ Bro∴ D. R. MUNRO, that the Grand Commander's address be referred to a special committee to recommend what action shall be taken thereon.

The Sov∴ Grand Commander appointed the following :— Ill∴ Bros∴ J. V. ELLIS, W. H. HUTTON, and WM. B. SIMPSON.

The Supreme Council was called from labor at 1.10 o'clock.

The Supreme Council resumed labor at 2.35 o'clock.

Ill∴ Bro∴ D. B. TRACY, of Detroit, Michigan, the Grand Representative of this Council near the Sup∴ Co∴ of the Northern Jurisdiction of the U. S., was admitted and welcomed.

In accordance with the notice given at the session in 1878, it was moved by Ill∴ Bro∴ MURTON, seconded by Ill∴ Bro∴ MACKAY, that article 15, paragraph 2, of the statutes relating to fees and dues be altered as follows—that the words " from a Chapter of Rose Croix, seven dollars," be expunged and the following substituted, viz, " from a Chapter of Rose Croix, covering a Lodge of Perfection and Council of Princes of Jerusalem, *seven dollars*, and from a Chapter of Rose Croix, covering a Council of Princes of Jerusalem, *four dollars*."— Carried.

REPORTS OF SPECIAL DEPUTIES.

The following Reports were read :—

PROVINCE OF QUEBEC.

OFFICE OF THE DEPUTY

FOR THE PROVINCE OF QUEBEC,

MONTREAL, 6th Oct., 1879.

To the Supreme Council, 33°, A∴ & A∴ S∴ R∴ for the Dominion of Canada.

ILLUSTRIOUS BRETHREN :—

Once more the pleasing duty devolves upon me of tendering to you my annual statement of the condition and working of the Ancient and Accepted Scottish Rite in the Province of Quebec, over which, by your kindness, I hold the supervision.

I am happy to say that I have nothing but peace and harmony to record.

The various Bodies are progressing satisfactorily, and if slowly, at the same time surely and with a due regard to the quality of the material they work upon.

I have visited Hochelaga Lodge of Perfection frequently during the year, and I am greatly pleased to report that Ill∴ Bro∴ C. G. GEDDES, 32°, its present head, is a most indefatigable and painstaking worker, and that in his hands our glorious ritual loses none of its beauty and power.

Ill∴ Bro∴ A. D. NELSON, the recently elected most wise Sovereign of Hochelaga Chapter of Rose Croix, has not yet got to work, but I anticipate under the new executive, a fresh impulse, and now that each Body has its own separate head the result cannot but be beneficial, as each will be enabled to devote the whole of his energy to the Body over which he holds control.

I regret extremely that owing to the peculiar position occupied by Masonry in this Province, surrounded as it is by a hostile people, I have been unable to carry out the views of the Supreme Council by planting Lodges of Perfection in in other places than Montreal.

As, however, there are at last appearances that we are about to emerge from the long period of depression that has damped our energies, I trust not only will the accessions to our ranks be more numerous, but that other cities in the Province will catch our enthusiasm and help us to carry on the good work.

The whole respectfully and fraternally submitted,

WM. H. HUTTON, 33°,

Deputy, Province of Quebec.

PROVINCE OF ONTARIO.

OFFICE OF THE DEPUTY,

HAMILTON, Oct. 8th, 1879.

To the Sov∴ Grand Commander and Members of the Supreme Council, 33°, for the Dominion of Canada.

ILL∴ BRETHREN :—

I have much pleasure in submitting a report for the year now ended of the condition of the Rite in the jurisdiction entrusted to my supervision.

The various Bodies in Hamilton, Toronto and London are all in a prosperous and flourishing condition, showing no diminution in work, but on the contrary, an increase in membership and in zeal and earnestness, peace and harmony prevailing among all.

During the past year I have (in accordance with the power entrusted to the Special Deputies at the last session), entered into correspondence with several cities and towns in my Province, and the result has been that now there are parties in several places actively engaged in getting the statutory number together with a view of opening a Lodge of Perfection in each city. I have also been applied to from Manitoba, by a number of the best members of the Craft in that far off Province, praying that a Deputy of this Council be sent there to confer the degrees and open a Lodge of Perfection in the City of Winnipeg (the correspondence in connection therewith I will now read). It will, therefore, lay with this council to decide what action shall be taken to comply with the request, and occupy that prosperous and promising field.   The Council will, therefore, see that although no new Bodies have actually been formed, there is good ground for believing that, with the reviving state of trade and consequently better feeling, a number of Bodies in the West will very shortly be opened, and this system of Masonry be extended and propagated.

In the City of Hamilton, the past winter, the members of the Rite, in anti-cipation of the visit of the Supreme Council, at its Special Session, caused meetings to be called in each branch, at the request of some the Illustrious 33rds, for the purpose of exemplifying the degrees, but their disappointment was great when they found that scarcely a member was present, and that, although they had pre-pared an entertainment and had taken the trouble of having day as well as evening sessions, with foreign visitors and those from Sister Bodies present to welcome them, like the parable of the man "marrying a wife," all or nearly all "could not come." However, they were gratified and delighted, as they always are, at having our revered Sov.·. Gr.·. Commander, as well Ill.·. Bro.·. SIMPSON, present, and the work of Perfection, Chapter and Consistory, was done in a manner to meet their hearty approval.

In this connection the members of the Rite in the City of Hamilton intend to follow out the practice which obtains in various places in the Northern Jurisdic-tion of the U. S. and have "annual reunions," to confer all the degrees from the 4° to the 32°, thereby gathering together a large number of the Brethren of the Dominion and the jurisdictions over the border, promoting the interchange of ideas, inspiring zeal in their own members and affording an opportunity for the exchange of fraternal greetings and the extending of courtesies. In mentioning this, your Deputy asks for the Hamilton Brethren the countenance of the members of this Supreme Council, and submits the scheme of the proposed reunions for their approval.

The Toronto Brethren, this summer, in order to promote more social inter-course between the members of the Rite, got up a steamboat excursion solely for their members and families, which was a great success and must (as all such entertainments do), tend to the accomplishment of much good in the direction sought.

The London Brethren also (in anticipation of my official visit, with visitors from Hamilton), prepared for an excursion on the River Thames and generally to have a good time, but were disappointed by my failing (from illness in my family) to attend, which I exceedingly regret.

All this goes to show that the sentiments prevailing among the members of the Rite in this Province is of the right stamp, and that such fraternity of feeling being predominant among them gives us every assurance of the increasing pros-perity and popularity of this branch of the great Masonic family.

Fraternally submitted.

J. W. MURTON, 33°,
Deputy for Ontario.

PROVINCE OF NEW BRUNSWICK.

OFFICE OF THE DEPUTY FOR THE

PROVINCE OF NEW BRUNSWICK,

ST. JOHN, OCTOBER, 1879.

To the Supreme Council of the A∴ & A∴ S∴ R∴ for the Dominion of Canada.

GREETING :—

Although neither the Lodge of Perfection, Chapter of Rose Croix, nor the Consistory of this Jurisdiction have done a large amount of work during the past year, I am gratified to be enabled to record the fact that very material progress has been made in the true interests of the Ancient and Accepted Scottish Rite in the Province of New Brunswick. As regards the Lodge of Perfection, I may say that the fourth and fifth Degrees have been worked in extenso and that the other Degrees which have been conferred in the Lodge of Perfection as well as in the Chapter of Rose Croix and in the Consistory have been conferred in full, and that notwithstanding the disadvantages which we labor under, in consequence of the great fire of 1877, marked progress has been made by the respective officers in acquiring an accurate knowledge of our Ritual.

The meetings during the past year have alternated between the Masonic Hall in Carleton, on the western side of the harbor, and the new Masonic Temple recently erected by the New Brunswick Masonic Hall Company upon the spacious site owned by the said Company upon Germain Street in this City. This building when completed will cost about $80,000, and provision is being made for ample acccommodation for the several Bodies of our Order ; indeed, I may say that when fully completed, our new building for adaptability to the requirements of our brotherhood will not be second to any Masonic Temple in this Dominion.

In closing this brief report, allow me to express my deep regret that circumstances over which I have no control, present my being at the Grand East during this communication of our Supreme Council.

Respectfully submitted,

ROBERT MARSHALL, 33°,

Deputy for the Province of N. B.,
and Lieut. Gr∴ Com∴

On motion made by Ill∴ Bro∴ STEARNS, seconded by Ill∴ Bro∴ MACKAY, the above reports were referred to the committee on the doings of Special Deputies.

The Ill∴ Grand Chancellor presented his report, as follows :—

To the Supreme Council for the Dominion of Canada :

My official acts as Grand Chancellor have been few.

By direction of the Secretary General I transmitted Ill.·. Brother JOHN-FITZHENRY TOWNSEND, Ill.·. Brother JOSIAH H. DRUMMOND, Ill.·. Brother ALBERT PIKE, their diplomas of Honorary Membership in this Supreme Council. In consequence of the change of residence of Ill.·. Brother HAMILTON, of the English Supreme Council, his diploma still remains in my possession.

I have applied to the Supreme Council in England for information as to its views respecting the status and regularity of the Supreme Council for Egypt, but I feel bound to say that the application was made too late to enable the information to be obtained for use at the present Session of Supreme Council.

I have received (see letter of Ill.·. Brother RAMSDEN, appendix B.,) and transmitted to Ill.·. Brother REID, his exequator as representative of the Supreme Council for Colon, near this Supreme Council.

I also received (see letter of Ill.·. Brother DELACRETAZ, appendix C.,) and transmitted to Ill.·. Brother HUTTON, his exequator as representative of the Supreme Council of Switzerland, near this Supreme Council.

A very cordial letter sent me by Ill.·. Brother CHATTERTON, our representative near the Supreme Council for Ireland is appended (marked D).

A communication has been received by me from the Supreme Council of Brazil, announcing that Ill.·. Brother MACEDO had presented his credentials as our representative, and had been received with due honors ; that Ill.·. Brother STEARNS had been appointed as the representative of that Supreme Council near this, and enclosing his exequator, (see letter appendix E.)

Informally I have communicated with a number of Illustrious Brethren abroad, and I have, as Grand Chancellor, received printed papers and documents, which are, for the most part, dealt with by the Committee on Foreign Relations.

JOHN V. ELLIS, 33°,
Grand Chancellor.

On motion, the above report was received and laid upon the table.

Ill.·. Bro.·. TRACY, of the Northern Supreme Council of the U. S. A., retired.

The Committee on the Doings of Subordinate Bodies, who had had the returns in their possession for inspection, presented their report, as follows :—

To the M∴ P∴ Sov∴ Grand Commander and Illustrious Brethren of the Supreme Council, 33°, of the A∴ & A∴ S∴ Rite, Dominion of Canada.

Your Committee on "Doings of Subordinate Bodies" beg to report as follows:—

PROVINCE OF NEW BRUNSWICK.

ST. JOHN.

NEW BRUNSWICK CONSISTORY has done no work during the year. Membership, 37 ; fees to Supreme Council, $9.50. Died, one—Bro∴ JAS. SCOVIL.

HARINGTON CHAPTER OF ROSE CROIX conferred the 16° on two, and the 18° on two Brethren. Membership, 66 ; fees to Supreme Council, $30.75. Died, one—Bro∴ JAS. SCOVIL.

ST. JOHN LODGE OF PERFECTION conferred the 14° on two Brethren. Membership, 61 ; fees to Supreme Council, 21.25.

PROVINCE OF NOVA SCOTIA.

HALIFAX.

KEITH CHAPTER ROSE CROIX, covering Lodge of Perfection, have made no returns for the present year.

PROVINCE OF ONTARIO.

HAMILTON.

MOORE SOVEREIGN CONSISTORY conferred the 30° on eight, 31° on four, 32° on ten. Membership, 71 ; fees to Supreme Council, $112.75.

HAMILTON CHAPTER OF ROSE CROIX conferred the 16° on five and the 18° on nine Brethren. Membership, 80; fees to Supreme Council, $40.25.— Died—one, Ill∴ Brother ARCHIBALD MACALLUM, 31°.

MURTON LODGE OF PERFECTION conferred the 14° on thirteen Brethren. Membership, 105 ; fees to Supreme Council, $59.25.—Died—one, Ill∴ Brother ARCHIBALD MACALLUM.

LONDON.

LONDON CHAPTER OF ROSE CROIX, covering Lodge of Perfection, conferred the 14° on four, 16° on four and 18° on four Brethren. Membership, 48 ; fees to Supreme Council, $54.25.—Died—one, P∴ M∴ W∴ S∴, WM. S. SMITH, 18°.

TORONTO.

TORONTO CHAPTER OF ROSE CROIX conferred the 16° on five and the 18° on seven Brethren. Membership, 53 ; fees to Supreme Council, $42.00.— Members withdrawn, three.

TORONTO LODGE OF PERFECTION conferred the 14° on seven Brethren. Membership, 67 ; fees to Supreme Council, $41.75. Members withdrawn, four.

PROVINCE OF QUEBEC.

MONTREAL.

MONTREAL CONSISTORY conferred the 31° on two and the 32° on two Brethren.   Membership, 42 ; fees to Supreme Council, $20.75.   Withdrawn, 3. Suspended, 1.

HOCHELAGA CHAPTER OF ROSE CROIX conferred the 16° on three and the 18° on three Brethren.   Membership, 49 ; fees to Supreme Council, $34.25. Withdrawn, 5.

HOCHELAGA LODGE OF PERFECTION conferred the 14° on ten Brethren. Membership, 55 ; fees to Supreme Council, $33.00.   Withdrawn, 5.

Respectfully and fraternally submitted,

H. A. MACKAY, 33°,

Chairman.

HAMILTON, ONT., 7th October, 1879.

On motion of Ill.·. Bro.·. MACKAY, seconded by Ill.·. Bro.·. MOORE, the above report was received and laid upon the table.

The Supreme Council took a recess from 4 o'clock to 4.30 o'clock, and upon resuming,

The Committee on the Grand Commander's Address presented the following report :—

The Committee share the regret of the Sovereign Grand Commander that so few of the Members of the Supreme Council were able to be present at the Special Session held at Hamilton, in March last.   The occasion was one of great interest to the Supreme Council itself ; and the Hamilton Brethren had prepared for it with even more than their usual zeal and energy. . The illustration of the work of the Rite would have carried instruction to the different parts of the country where the Inspectors General reside, had they availed themselves of it, and the meeting would have ever been a pleasant remembrance to all who joined in it.   To a large extent, however, the presence of the Sovereign Grand Commander saved the credit of the Supreme Council, and the Committee are satisfied that the warm language in which the labors and the hospitality of the Hamilton Brethren are commended in the address, is just and well deserved.

The Committee note with satisfaction that the Sovereign Grand Commander has issued few dispensations to waive the statutory period of time for conferring the Degrees.   Cases will always arise when the exercise of the dispensing power is justifiable, and in safe hands the judicious exercise of that power must prove beneficial.

The Committee recommend that so much of the address as relates to Foreign Supreme Councils, be referred to the Committee on Foreign Relations ; that the portion relating to changes in the titles of officers be referred to the Committee on Ritual, to report at the next Annual Session, or as soon as convenient ; and that the Confession of Faith submitted by the Sovereign Grand Commander be referred to the same Committee.

The Supreme Council will share in the regret of the Committee, that the Sovereign Grand Commander was unable to avail himself of the courteous invitation to attend the Session of the Supreme Council for the Northern Jurisdiction of the United States, lately held at Philadelphia. The fraternal relations, the kind feelings which exist between the two Supreme Councils would be strengthened by such a visit, and from our Illustrious Brethren of the Rite in the United States, the Sovereign Grand Commander would receive a hearty and generous welcome.

We are under never-ending obligation to Illustrious Brother ALBERT PIKE, Sovereign Grand Commander of the Southern Jurisdiction of the United States, and each Session we learn of something that adds to the weight of unrequited service he has rendered us. A magnificent array of books, the result of his years of profound study and the product of his brilliant genius, already enriches the archives of the Supreme Council, and to this at the present Session other additions are made. We know no means by which we can repay our Illustrious Brother, but we lay at his feet our tribute of respect for his learning, and of our love and gratitude for the kindness he is continually showing us. To him special thanks are due this year for his letter in answer to certain Masons in Ontario, questioning the authority of this Supreme Council, submitted by the Sovereign Grand Commander with his address, which your Committee recommend to be printed with the proceedings, as an evidence of the courteous and effective manner in which our Illustrious Brother deals with those who questioned the regularity of one of his most important acts in connection with the Rite, viz :—The inauguration of this Supreme Council.

The Supreme Council having in previous years discussed fully the question of uniting in the Lausanne Convention and in the Concilier League, and having reached the conclusion that it would be wise to remain untrammelled by any alliance except that which is based on a good understanding, the outcome of fraternal correspondence, your Committee do not deem it advisable to make any further recommendation to the Supreme Council upon this subject. With regard to that portion of the articles of the League to which the Sovereign Grand Commander calls special attention, viz :—" That no person can ever be recognized as lawfully invested with any degree of the Ancient and Accepted Scottish Rite, by having received a degree claiming to be such, as part of any other Rite," the Committee need only remark that this is so well understood in this Jurisdiction that it does not seem possible for any one to be recognized of any degree of the Ancient and Accepted Scottish Rite, unless he shall have legally and lawfully received that degree in the Rite. In the judgment of the Committee, therefore, no amendment of the statutes is necessary to meet what may be considered an impossible case, and the Committee so advise the Supreme Council.

Your Committee learn with much satisfaction that the misunderstanding existing at Toronto last year, has been amicably settled.   It is more pleasant to record the existence of harmony, than to enter upon disputes.   At best throughout the Dominion we are a small family, and we should live happily and harmoniously, evincing in our lives the moral teachings of the Masonic profession.

Your Committee hear with pleasure that application for the establishment of Bodies of the Rite have been received from several districts in the West, and they have no doubt that in the hands of the Illustrious Deputy for Ontario, under the Sovereign Grand Commander, the Lodge of Perfection at the places indicated will, if established, soon show evidence that this beautiful Rite is appreciated by all who enter it.

With the Sovereign Grand Commander your Committee mourn the death of Brothers at Hamilton, and at St. John and at London ; but they feel grateful that of our numbers so few have received their last summons, and are finally separated from us on earth.   The circle of the Supreme Council itself remains unbroken, and although the Sovereign Grand Commander utters a warning that time is fleeting in reminding us that he has passed the allotted three-score years and ten, we may be permitted to hope that he will be spared for many years to preside over our deliberations, to moderate our judgments, and to guide aright our decisions, and by his genial, kindly nature to draw us closer and closer in the bonds of fraternal love.   In his hope we most cordially unite : that we may all be spared until next year to renew our labors and to meet and greet each other, and may our Father who is in Heaven, keep us and bless us.

Respectfully submitted,

JOHN V. ELLIS, 33°,
W. H. HUTTON, 33°,
W. B. SIMPSON, 33°.

On motion made by Ill∴ Bro∴ ELLIS, seconded by Ill∴ Bro∴ MACKAY, the report was received and adopted.

The Secretary General presented several valuable works as presents from the Supreme Council of the Southern Jurisdiction of the U. S., through the very Illustrious Brother ALBERT PIKE ; and, on motion made by Ill∴ Bro∴ MUNRO, seconded by Ill∴ Bro∴ ELLIS, the Secretary General was instructed to convey to Ill∴ Bro∴ PIKE the hearty thanks of this Supreme Council for the works just mentioned, as well, also, for his uniform kindness and generosity displayed towards this Supreme Council.

The Special Committee on Ritual read their final report, which was as follows :—

MONTREAL, October 8th, 1879.

To the Supreme Council, 33º, for the Dominion of Canada.

ILL.˙. BRETHREN :—

Your Special Committee on Ritual have much pleasure in presenting the Council with their final report, and submitting the ceremonials for inaugurating and constituting Lodges of Perfection, Chapters of Rose Croix and Consistories of S.˙. P.˙. R.˙. S.˙. with the installation of their officers, as also the forms for "dedicating Halls of the Rite, and holding funerals and Lodges of Sorrow."

Their labor in these, as in a great part of their work since their appointment, has been but comparatively little, as they have had a never-failing source to apply to in the extensive, complete and magnificent works of that prince of Masonic authors and compilers, ALBERT PIKE, to whom we are indebted for a large portion of that which we have presented to this Council, our work consisting principally in abbreviating and revising to suit the Canadian system, we therefore, trust that our labors, although imperfect in many respects, will be accepted.

JOHN W. MURTON, 33°, ⎫
　　　　　　　　　　　　　　　⎬ *Committee.*
WM. H. HUTTON, 33°, ⎭

In accordance with the notice given at the Special Session, in March, the question of the recognition of the Supreme Council of Egypt came up, when it was moved by Ill.˙. Bro.˙. HUTTON, seconded by Ill.˙. Bro.˙. STEARNS, that the subject of the recognition of the Supreme Council of Egypt be left in the hands of the Sov.˙. Gr.˙. Commander, to deal with as he may deem best.—Carried.

The following resolution, moved by Ill.˙. Bro.˙. ELLIS, seconded by Ill.˙. Bro.˙. SIMPSON, was then adopted :—

Resolved,—That the work of preparing the Rituals, Forms of Installation and other Ceremonials for the use of Bodies of the Rite in Canada being now completed, the Supreme Council desires to place upon record its sense of the diligence, zeal and ability which the Illustrious Brothers MURTON and HUTTON brought to the discharge of their duties as a Ritual Committee, and an expression of its satisfaction at the thoroughness and effectiveness of the work accomplished by them.

Further Resolved,—That the Sovereign Grand Commander be requested to convey to these Illustrious Brethren the thanks of the Supreme Council for their valuable services as the Ritual Committee.

Letters and other documents from the following Foreign

Supreme Councils, viz :—of France, Mexico, Brazil, Belgium, Northern Jurisdiction U. S. A., and the Southern Jurisdiction U. S. A., were read by the Secretary General, and, on motion, were referred to the Committee on Foreign Relations and Correspondence.

The Council was called from labor at 5.30 o'clock.

THURSDAY, October 9th, 1879.

The Supreme Council resumed labor at 11 o'clock A. M.

Ill∴ Bro∴ T. D. HARINGTON,
Sov∴ Gr∴ Commander.

"   "   WILLIAM H. HUTTON,
As Lieut∴ Gr∴ Commander.

"   "   JOHN W. MURTON,
Secretary General.

"   "   HUGH A. MACKAY,
Treasurer General.

"   "   JOHN V. ELLIS,
Grand Chancellor.

"   "   DAVID R. MUNRO,
As Gr∴ Captain of the Guard.

The Deputy for Ontario presented a petition from a number of members of the Craft in Manitoba asking that a Deputy of this Supreme Council be sent to the City of Winnipeg, for the purpose of organizing a Lodge of Perfection. Letters also with reference to the above were read.

It was then moved by Ill∴ Bro∴ HUTTON, seconded by Ill∴ Bro∴ ELLIS, that the petition be granted, and that it be left with the Sov∴ Grand Commander and the Secretary General to carry the same into execution.—Carried.

Ill∴ Bro∴ WM. H. HUTTON, as the representative of the Supreme Council of Switzerland, and Ill∴ Bro∴ ISAAC H.

STEARNS, as the representative of the Supreme Council of Brazil, presented their credentials and were heartily welcomed.

Ill.·. Bro.·. GEORGE O. TYLER, the Deputy of the Supreme Council of the N.·. J.·. U. S., for the State of Vermont, was announced, admitted and welcomed.

Ill.·. Bro.·. TYLER responded to the Grand Commander's welcome in eloquent terms.

The Committee on Foreign Relations presented their Annual Report, as follows :—

ENGLAND.

There have been some changes in the Supreme Council. Our Illustrious Representative at that Supreme Council, Bro.·. HAMILTON, has removed to the West Indies, and has vacated his seat as an active member. The Supreme Council as now constituted consists of

GRAND PATRON.

HIS ROYAL HIGHNESS ALBERT EDWARD PRINCE OF WALES.

HONORARY MEMBERS.

HIS ROYAL HIGHNESS ARTHUR, DUKE OF CONNAUGHT.
HIS ROYAL HIGHNESS PRINCE LEOPOLD.

THE COUNCIL.

LORD SKELMERSDALE, *Sov.·. Grand Commander.*
CAPT. NATHANIEL GEORGE PHILLIPS, *Lt.·. Grand Commander.*
MAJOR GENERAL HENRY CLERKE, *Grand Treasurer General.*
JOHN MONTAGU PULTNEY MONTAGU, *Grand Chancellor.*
LT.-COLONEL SHADWELL HENRY CLERKE, *Grand Secretary General.*
HUGH DAVID SANDEMAN, *Grand Secretary for Foreign Correspondence.*
SIR MICHAEL COSTA, *Grand Captain of the Guards.*
COL. ALEXANDER WILLIAM ADAIR, *Sov.·. Gd.·. Ins.·. General.*
GENERAL JOHN STUDHOLME BROWNRIGG, *Sov.·. Gd.·. Ins.·.,General.*

Dr. ROBERT HAMILTON, at present member, residing in the West Indies.

So far as your Committee are aware, no event of importance has transpired in the Rite in England the present year.

SCOTLAND.

There have been some changes in the Supreme Council for Scotland since the last report of the Committee, and that Illustrious body is now constituted as follows :—

JOHN WHYTE MELVILLE, *Sov.·. Gd.·. Commander.*

THE RT. HON. THE EARL OF ROSSLYN, *Lt.·. Gd.·. Commander.*

LINDSAY MACKERSY, W.S., *Ill.·. Secretary General.*

WILLIAM MANN, S.S.C., *Ill.·. Treasurer General.*

COL. A. CAMPBELL CAMPBELL, *Ill.·. G.·. M.·. C.·.*

SIR MICHAEL R. SHAW STEWART, *Ill.·. G.·. C.·. G.·.*

THE RT. HON. THE EARL OF MAR AND KILLIE, *Ill.·. G.·. Standard Bearer.*

SIR MOLYNEUX HYDE NEPEAN, *Ill.·. G.·. Sword Bearer.*

THE RT. HON. LORD INVERURIE, *Ill.·. G.·. Archivist.*

The Supreme Council has upon its roll four honorary members, and one brother of the 33° in China, three in India, and two in New Zealand. One retired Insp.·. General, Ill.·. Bro.·. THOMAS ELDER MACRITCHIE, who still retained a warm interest in the Rite, died during the year. A warrant has been issued to a Rose Croix Chapter at Brisbane, Queensland. There are now upon the roll eight Chapters 18°, and five Consistories 30°. Fraternal relations have been entered into with the Supreme Council for Egypt ; and a decided expression of opinion has been given against the formation of a Supreme Council for New Zealand, or any other British Colony. The Supreme Council has also adopted the following :—

Whereas, certain spurious and unrecognized degrees in Masonry are being conferred on Brethren in Scotland, which tend to bring the legitimate orders into disrepute, it be resolved :—

First—That at Meetings or Festivals of the Supreme Council of Scotland or of any Lodge, Chapter, College, Senate, Areopagus, Tribunal, Council, or Consistory holding Charter therefrom, no one shall wear the Badge, Jewel, or Decoration of any degree or order which has not been conferred on him by a body whose title to give it is recognized by the Supreme Council ; and in event of any one transgressing this rule, and persisting in doing so after warning from the Chair, he shall, by order of the presiding Officer, be excluded from the Meeting.

Second—That for the purpose of the foregoing resolution, the following shall be recognized as lawfully entitled to wear the Badges, Jewels, or Decorations of their respective degrees :—

(1.) Any Master Mason admitted to the craft degrees in a Lodge holding of the Grand Lodge of Scotland, or of any Lodge holding of a Grand Lodge recognized by the Grand Lodge of Scotland.

(2.) Any Royal Arch Companion admitted to the degrees in a Chapter holding of the Supreme Grand Royal Arch Chapter of

Scotland, or in any Chapter holding of a Grand Chapter recognized by the Supreme Chapter of Scotland.

(3.) Any Member of the Royal Order of Scotland admitted either by the Grand Lodge of the Order, or any Provincial Grand Lodge.

(4.) Any Knight of the Red Cross of Constantine, Holy Sepulchre, and St. John, made in any Conclave or Sanctuary holding of the Grand Imperial Council of Scotland, or in any conclave or Sanctuary holding of any Grand Council recognized by the Grand Imperial Council of Scotland.

(5.) Any Knight Templar, Companion, or Commander admitted by any Priory or Encampment holding of the Chapter General of the Religious and Military Order of the Temple for Scotland, or of any Priory or Encampment holding of a Grand Priory or Encampment recognized by the Chapter General of Scotland.

(6.) Any Member of the Ancient and Accepted Scottish Rite admitted in any Lodge, Chapter, College, Senate, Areopagus, Tribunal, Council, or Consistory holding of, or in the Supreme Council for Scotland itself, or in any Lodge, Chapter, College, Senate, Areopagus, Tribunal, Council, or Consistory holding of, or in a Supreme Council of the 33d and Last Degree of the Ancient and Accepted Scottish Rite recognized by the Supreme Council of Scotland.

There appears to be no change in the relations between this Supreme Council and that for England.

IRELAND.

The Sovereign Grand Commander for the Supreme Council for Ireland, Ill.·. Bro.·. JOHN FITZHENRY TOWNSHEND, in an interesting address delivered to his Supreme Council at its last Annual Session thus refers to several matters connected with the Rite in that country :—

" You are all aware that this Council has existed for more than fifty years. It was in fact the first Council of the Thirty-third Degree established in the British Islands. But it has never attempted to exercise any authority outside this kingdom save on one single occasion, when it authorized the establishment of a Supreme Council for Portugal, which has since become merged in the Grande Oriente Lusitano of Lisbon. Even within the limits of Ireland it was for many years quite inactive. It was regarded even by its own members merely as a dignified body, to which it was some distinction to belong, but which had no duties to fulfil. Its early records are singularly devoid of interest ; it seems to have met only to admit new members as vacancies occurred, so as to keep up the original number of nine, to which it is still limited. But since it has been acknowledged as a governing body by those Degrees which are now admittedly subject to its authority, it has become more important, and within the last ten years its correspondence with other Councils of the Thirty-third Degree has become worth attention. I presume it had originally a right to establish subordinate bodies in any British Colony or Dependency. I am, however, of opinion that if so, the non-user of that right for so long a period must now be taken as evidence that the right itself has either been extinguished or been conceded to one or other or both of the other British Councils. The Supreme Council. for England and Wales now claims exclusive jurisdiction over the Dependencies of the British Crown. The Supreme Council for Scotland disputes that exclusive right, and claims co-ordinate and co-extensive powers in the British possessions abroad. This has led to a sharp contention, which has brought on an estrangement between those sister Councils, and the cessation of amicable relations between them. The arguments on both sides of this question have been laid before the Councils of the world ; it would be impossible not to form an opinion on the subject, but as we are not called on to decide the question, I prefer not to offer any views of my own about it Happily the dispute has not affected our position with respect to either of those Councils, and we continue, I rejoice to say, on the most friendly terms with both. And I earnestly recommend this Council not to assert a right which, if not extinguished, it would be both useless and mischievous to exercise in the present day.

"It is true that a Rose Croix chapter was for many years held at Lisbon under an Irish warrant, but not issued by our Supreme Council. It was issued by the "Council of Rites," established in 1846. Our Supreme Council has never exercised authority over the Rose Croix Degree in Ireland or elsewhere ; partly because Rose Croix chapters, which were or assumed to be independent, had been established in Ireland before our Supreme Council was formed ; partly because the Council of Rites had assumed the functions of a Supreme Council, and thus had thrown into obscurity the Council of the Thirty-third Degree founded here twenty years before. My own opinion of these matters is that the Freemasons of Ireland were, in those days, somewhat ignorant of the nature of the A∴ and A∴ S∴ Rite. However that may be, it seems unquestionable that the ideas entertained by some of them about the paramount eminence and importance of the Rose Croix Degree caused that and all the higher Degrees to be regarded with jealousy, and even with hostile feelings, as if they were inimical to the simplicity of what was called Ancient Masonry. All these causes combined to prevent our Supreme Council from being able, even if so disposed, to assume its proper position. The independence of the Rose Croix Degree in Ireland has caused great surprise elsewhere I have been often asked how it was possible that in a country where the A∴ and A∴ Rite was practised, and a Council of the Thirty third Degree established, the Rose Croix Degree (the eighteenth of the series) should not be subject to the Thirty-third Council. The fact that it is not so was long unknown or unregarded in other places. But a great change has taken place since the multiplication of Masonic periodicals and journals, and the circulation of the very able addresses and reports contained in the proceedings of the Councils for both Jurisdictions of the United States. Many who formerly were hardly aware of the existence of our Council are now anxious to hear of its history and its proceedings. I thought it my duty candidly to state these facts to the convocation of the Rose Croix Degree in June last, and I stated my individual opinion, in which I am glad to find many others concur, that it would be possible to make our system accord with that of every other country where the A.·. and A.·. Rite is practised, by making the Council of Thirty-third the supreme power of the Rose Croix Degree, yet retaining the Grand Chapter as an administrative body ; preserving all its really important functions, as well as the dignity of its officers, and leaving it, of course, the full control over its own funds. But nothing has been done in that direction, and the Rose Croix Degree, to its own disadvantage, as well as that of the Supreme Council, still retains its anomalistic and unrecognized position. I expressed to the Convocation my opinion that the subject would soon be forced on the attention of the Rose Croix Degree ; and I find that since I presented that Report the subject was alluded to in an address delivered on 17th September last, by the M.·. P.·. Grand Commander of the Northern Jurisdiction of the United States to his assembled Council. He expressed his opinion that there is now some danger that the organization of the Rite in Ireland will become such that Masons of that obedience cannot be recognized in other countries— an opinion for which, so far as the Rose Croix Degree is concerned, I fear there is some foundation. He adds—" It is certainly very desirable that our Irish Brethren should make their system conform to that in other jurisdictions." Those few words are of much weight, coming as they do from one so cautious, wise and deliberate ; who is as careful in forming his opinions as he is eloquent in expressing, and firm in defending them."

The domestic relations of the Supreme Council are in good condition, and its foreign relations pleasant and harmonious. Referring to the Supreme Council for Canada, our Illustrious Brother says :—

" We had the pleasure of admitting during the past year, COL. W. J. BURY MACLEOD MOORE, a member of the Supreme Council of Canada as an Honorary member of this Council, as a token on our part that we had not forgotten the connection of that estimable gentleman with Ireland and Irish Masonry, and were anxious to maintain our relations with Canada, which have always been most cordial, and I trust will continue to be so."

It may be of interest to append another paragraph from Bro.·. TOWNSHEND'S address to show how rigidly the Supreme Council for Switzerland regards the matter of communication and exchange of representatives with those Supreme Councils not in the Lausanne Convention :—

" The Supreme Council for Switzerland, with which we had formerly been on friendly terms, did me the honor some years since of naming me as its representative with you. The Letters of Credence were handed to me by our late Secretary-General. After his death I found among his official papers a letter in the French language, relative to that appointment, to which as it seemed to me no answer had been given. I therefore wrote to the M.·. P. . Br.·. Besançon. whom I believed to be the Commander of the S.·. C.·. for Switzerland, stating the long illness and death of the late Secretary-General ; our own desire to revive our amicable correspondence, and excusing, as well as I could, the omission to answer the letter of the Swiss Council. I received a very gentlemanlike and courteous reply from our very highly respected Brother Besançon, stating that he had ceased to command the Council, but had consulted it respecting my letter ; and had found that before renewing friendly relations with us, it would require our adhesion to the Confederation of Lausanne. He added that the Swiss Council was the executive power (*pouvoir executif*) of that Confederation, and would be happy to communicate to the other Councils belonging to it our desire to join it ; but that unless we should express that desire, the S.·. C.·. for Switzerland could not respond to our intentions.

" I replied that we were an independent Council ; that we sought no favor from any other, and did not mean to make any submission whatever, however pleased we should have been had our well-meant offer met a different reception ; and since we have not joined the Confederation of Lausanne, and have no intention of doing so, we must remain as we are with regard to the Council for Switzerland."

The Illustrious Brother consoles himself with the reflection that " our correspondence is of the most friendly and fraternal character with the five great " English speaking Councils of the world."

The " organization" of the Rite in Ireland differs from its organization in the other countries in which it prevails. The number of members of the Supreme Council is limited to nine, and of the Thirty-second Grade to sixteen. There appears to be separate bodies of the 29th, 30th and 31st degrees. The Rose Croix is not under the immediate jurisdiction of the Supreme Council as will be seen by the extract given above. In regard to the 32°, the Sov.·. Grand Commander recommends that, although the members of that grade prefer to be under the Supreme Council rather than to have a separate Consistory, a distinct set of officers should be appointed for the degree, and "that the members should be regularly invited each year to attend our January meeting, which might, when its peculiar business was attended to, resolve itself into a Consistory of the 32°, so as to allow the Brethren to be present at the reading of the Report of the Commander."

The Sovereign Grand Commander of the Council in a Circular letter addressed to the bodies of its obedience and to its Foreign Representatives— a copy of which has been sent your Committee by Ill.·. Bro.·. DOMVILLE, 33°, announces the death of Ill.·. Bro.·. WILLIAM FETHERSTONHAUGH, 33°, (an active member of the Supreme Council), and pays an eloquent tribute to his Masonic virtues.

BELGIUM.

The Committee have received the Bulletin of the Supreme Council of Belgium covering its transactions from 1st November, 1877, to 1st November, 1878 ; a complete set of these transactions would be a most valuable addition to the Library of the Supreme Council if it could be obtained, and the Committee recommend that our Representative near that Supreme Council, Ill.·. Bro.·. CLUYDTS, be written to upon the subject.

The Supreme Council is composed of thirty active members, of whom Ill. ∴ Bro. ∴ Lieut. ∴ General RENARD is Sovereign Grand Commander, and Ill. ∴, Bro. ∴ LEOPOLD RICHE, Secretary-General. The oldest member is Brother JAWKS BRIEKMAN, who was created a Thirty-third in 1833. At its sitting, 18th March, 1878, this Supreme Council celebrated the sixty-first anniversary of its foundation, when the Grand Orator delivered a very interesting historical sketch of the Council, arguing that its past history was an honorable one, and justified the inference that its future would be brilliant. This Supreme Council does a great deal of work. Its Sessions are held at Brussels. It meets several times a year as a Supreme Council to transact the administrative business of the Rite, and at other times to confer the high grades, which it appears to do from the 22° to the 32°. It occupies itself with public questions, such as education, the improvement of man, and it aids important undertakings. At its sitting, on the 3rd August, 1878, it voted two hundred and fifty francs to aid in the erection of a public monument in the village of Ath, to the memory of F. DEFACQZ, President of the Court of Cassation, and one of the founders of the Belgium nationality, who had also been a distinguished and active Brother. At the sitting of 12th October, the President, in the absence of the Grand Commander, announced that an event of considerable importance had transpired since the last Session. This event was the resignation of a Ministry whose tendency he alleged was ultramontane and inimical to the Masonic institution. The new Ministry, he added, contained among its number, no less than three members of the Supreme Council ; the Sovereign Grand Commander, Bro. ∴ RENARD, was Minister of War ; the Lieutenant Grand Commander, Bro. ∴ VON HUMBEECK, Minister of Public Instruction ; and Bro. ∴ BARA, 32°, had been nominated Minister of Justice. It was an honor to which the Supreme Council could not be indifferent ; and therefore at an informal Convocation of the Supreme Council on 30th August, a deputation had been named to express the fraternal sentiment of their peers in the Supreme Council to the new Ministers, and to congratulate them upon the marks of public confidence with which they had been invested. All of the members of the Supreme Council joined in the deputation. They had waited upon the new Ministers, presented them with an address, and the Sovereign Grand Commander on his own behalf and that of his two associates thanked them for the courtesy and for this mark of their fraternal affection, and, at the same time, assured them that even though public duties might interfere with his attendance at Supreme Council, his interest in the work of the Rite would not cease. In the bodies subject to the Supreme Council, there is a very active spirit ; philosophical, educational, and other matters are discussed. In one Chapter an essay was read by a Brother on the employment of women in the mines. Other bodies had interested themselves in the work of succouring the unhappy people in the countries affected by the Eastern war. Subscriptions were taken up, concerts organized, and committees formed to send money, medicine, and clothes to the unhappy sufferers. There is an active philosophic and practical Masonic spirit at work in Belgium. The "transactions" contain a good review of Foreign Freemasonry, including the proceedings of our Supreme Council for 1877, which are courteously noticed.

The Committee have learned, by a circular dated 1st Aug., 1879 (appendix F), that Ill.·. Bro.·. RENARD, the Sov.·. Grand Commander of this Supreme Council died at Brussels, on 3rd July. This Brother was born in 1804, and had led a very active life. He joined in the movement for National Independence in 1830, and ever since that time had occupied a prominent position in the eye of the Belgium public, having filled several important military and civic functions, and was at the time of his death a Lieutenant-General in the Army and Minister of-War. " To a sound judgment," say our mourning Brethren of Belgium, " he united fervency with moderation. His heart was open to all generous thoughts, and to all those ideas of progress which appeared to him useful to humanity. By his activity, and by his labors, he had restored the Ancient and Accepted Scottish Rite to its former glory." The Committee recommend that a letter of condolence be sent to the Supreme Council of Belgium on the death of its venerable head.

MEXICO.

The Supreme Council for Mexico was established in 1814, and has had many vicissitudes. It appears always to have serious internal difficulties, chiefly owing to its control over the Symbolic Lodges. Three communications have been received from it the present year, one announcing the expulsion from all his Masonic rights and privileges of General D. LUIS MIER Y TERAN, Governor of the State of Veracruz. One announcing the death of the Ill.·. Brother ESTEBAN ZENTENO, Representative of the Supreme Council of the Southern Jurisdiction of the United States ; and the last, the filling of the vacancy caused by his death by the elevation to the grade of Bro.·. ALEJANDRO DEL PASO Y TRONCOSO. The Committee last year recommended the Supreme Council to enter into fraternal relations with the Supreme Council of Mexico, and this was agreed to, but no further action appears to have been taken. In his address the present year the Sov.·. Grand Commander explains why action has been delayed. With the action of the Supreme Council of Mexico in expelling Masons who seek to establish a system of Government for the three Degrees, we can have no sympathy whatever, and with the Sovereign Grand Commander we heartily accord that there should be a separate system of Government for those Degrees.. On the other hand it is well to remember that our view is not the view that generally prevails in the Latin Councils ; that in Mexico the Supreme Council has had control of all the Degrees ; and that the endeavor of certain Masons of the Scottish Rite in Mexico to establish Symbolic Lodges without the consent of the Supreme Council may appear to the Supreme Council an invasion of right and a violation of the obligation of fidelity ; we may wish it were otherwise ; we may kindly and cordially express our views on this subject without interfering further, and possibly the influence of our words and example may have a good influence. The matter is now in the hands of the Sovereign Grand Commander to act whenever he may deem it advisable.

The Committee acknowledge the receipt of several numbers of the *Bulletin of the Sov.·. Chap. Tenoch, No. 1,* an exclusively Masonic journal, published in the city of Mexico.

NORTHERN JURISDICTION U. S. A.

The Supreme Council for the Northern Jurisdiction of the United States of America, is now composed of about forty-five active members, vacancies occurring by death or otherwise not being filled, and it is contemplated to allow the number to be reduced to Thirty-three. At the Session held last month in Philadelphia, the honorary grade, 33°, was conferred on seventeen members of the 32°. At this Session, also, the Triennial election of officers was held with the following result : HENRY L. PALMER, Wisconsin, Sov.·. Grand Commander ; CHAS. L. WOODBURY, Mass., Lt.·. Grand Commander ; JAS. D. EVANS, New York, Grand Min.·. of State ; HEMON ELY, Ohio, Grand Treasurer ; CLINTON F. PAIGE, New York, Grand Secretary ; ALBERT P. MORIARTY, New York, Asst.·. Gd.·. Secretary ; SAMUEL. C. LAWRENCE, Mass., Gd.·. Keeper of the Archives ; CHAS. T. McCLENACHAN, N. Y., Gd.·. Master of Ceremonies ; H. STANLEY GOODWIN, Pa., Grand Marshal ; WM. R. HIGBY, Conn., Grand Standard Bearer ; GEO. O. TYLER, Vermont, Gd.·. Captain of the Guard ; THOS. R. LAMBERT, Mass., Grand Prior ; J. H. H. WARD, New York ; CHAS. C. MEYER, Pa., and HUGH McCURDY, Michigan, Gd.·. Marshals of the Camp.

Ill.·. Brother JOSIAH H. DRUMMOND absolutely declined a re-election. This Illustrious Brother had presided over the Supreme Council for twelve years, since, indeed, the union of what are commonly called the New York and Boston Councils. At the time of the union he was the Sov.·. Gr.·. Commander of the Council which then had its Grand East at Boston. He has discharged the duties of high station with great ability and with excellent judgment. His knowledge of the condition of the Rite in his own country and of its practices in foreign countries is very great, and your Committee have, on several occasions, been indebted to him for information promptly and courteously conveyed. As a presiding officer he was ready and decisive, and in the discharge of every duty, effective. That he should gladly seek rest from the active labors of the Chair is not surprising. His successor is a very eminent Mason, a learned jurist, and your Committee believe that our kindly relations with the Supreme Council for the Northern Jurisdiction U. S. A. will remain as cordial and pleasant under his rule as they were under that of Ill.·. Bro.·. DRUMMOND.

SOUTHERN JURISDICTION U. S. A.

The sessions of the Supreme Council for the Southern Masonic Jurisdiction of the United States are held every two years ; no session will be held the present year. The proposal to abolish the titles or (most of them), used in the Rite has been submitted to a vote of the members by circular, and has been sustained almost unanimously. No official copy of the changes made has been furnished your Committee, but they submit the copy sent by Ill.·. Bro.·. WEBBER to the Chairman for his private use. The proposition to substitute simpler titles for those now generally in use has met with favor in several Supreme Councils and, eventually, will be generally accepted. Something might be said in defence of the use of these titles, as to their giving roundness and finish in addressing the officers, as to their aid in promoting courtesy among the Brethren, as imparting dignity to our Assemblies, and as aids to creating a high sense of personal respect, individually, provided always that a true Masonic spirit underlies their use. On the other hand, it may be forcibly urged that they are inconsistent with the spirit of Masonic equality, that they are unnecessary, and that their appearance in the public newspapers and secular journals, attached to the names of simple and unobtrusive citizens, does not tend to dignify our institution in the eyes of the world. It is, however, no part of the duty of your Committee to make any recommendation to the Supreme Council in this matter. They merely record the action of a sister Supreme Council.

The Committee think that it would be interesting to the members of the Rite in Canada to print with the proceedings of the present year Ill.·. Bro.·. PIKE's views upon the connection with, and authority of the Supreme Council over, the Symbolic Degrees. Without adopting or dissenting from those views, the Committee think that it will be admitted by every member of the Rite, who calmly weighs the subject, that the attempts at control over the Symbolic Degrees by the Supreme Councils have been the prolific parent of disorder, confusion and bad feeling. It is, perhaps, natural for men everywhere to assume that the system of government which they have devised or chosen or created is the best system. It is natural, therefore, that we should prefer our own, and see in it many merits over foreign systems. Yet every dispassionate observer will admit that in countries like the United States and the Mother Land, where the Symbolic Lodges have representative government, and where they are not controlled by the Supreme Councils, there is far more harmony, better government and more satisfactory results than there is in those countries where there is a mixed system, or where the Supreme Council controls Symbolic Lodges, or where, as is unfortunately the case in some instances, the independence of the Supreme Council is merged in a "Grand Orient." Bro.·. PIKE's views show the growth of opinion in his own mind as to the authority of Supreme Councils over the degrees named, and are interesting reading. (See appendix G)

The condition of the Rite in the Southern States, and particularly in the Southwestern States, is excellent. There is marked progress in many directions and much to rejoice over.

The Supreme Council mourns the death of one of its active members, JOHN BURTON MAUDE, of the State of Missouri, who died on 29th April, 1879, aged 40 years, and who had been a member of the Supreme Council since 1874.

EGYPT.

The position of the Rite in Egypt is, that the Supreme Council having been regularized as legitimate by the Supreme Council for Italy, has been recognized as legitimate by the Supreme Council for the Southern Jurisdiction of the United States, by that of Ireland, of Scotland, of Greece, and perhaps by some other Supreme Councils. We might do the same, but as we have asked the views of the Supreme Council of England, it is at least courteous to await an answer. The Supreme Council for Egypt committed a grave irregularity in establishing a

Supreme Council for New Zealand, but it condoned that wrong as far as it was possible to do it. The matter of recognition might be left in the hands of the Sovereign Grand Commander, with power to act during the recess if he finds it necessary to do so.

The Supreme Council for Egypt appears to be composed of nineteen active members, but the Committee have no means of knowing the number of subordi. nate members. Its Bulletin gives as dependent upon it, a Grand Consistory, 32°, a Grand Tribune, 31°, Grand Areopagus, 30°, a Sovereign Chapter Rose Croix, 18°, and a Grand Body of the Royal Arch, 13°. It fraternizes with and, in a measure, appears to control the "Oriental Rite of Memphis," as officers of that Rite are also officers of the Supreme Council.

By Circular of 12th December, 1878, (appendix H), the names of three Brethren are transmitted to us, from among whom we may choose one as our representative.

BRAZIL.

The Committee have nothing of special importance to report from Brazil further than that the officers of the Supreme Council, for the five years 1879-84, were installed on 1st April, as follows :—

Ill.·. Bro.·. JOAQUIM SALDANHA MARINHO, *Grand Commander.*

BARON DE ST. FELIX, *Lieut.·. Grand Commander.*

ALEXANDRINO FREIRE DE AMARAL, *Grand Secretary.*

FRANCISCO JOSE DE LIMA BARROS, *Assistant Grand Secretary and Grand Chancellor.*

ANTONIO FRANCISCO GOULART, *Grand Treasurer.*

DOMINGOS DE AGEREDO CONTINTO DE DECQUE ESTRADA, *Grand Minister of State.*

ARISTIDES FELIX CÆSAR FARROUGH, *Grand Master of Ceremonies.*

JOXO D'ILLION L SILVA, *Grand Captain of the Guards.*

JOSE ANTONIO DA SILVA CARVALHO, *Grand Marshal of the Camp.*

There are two Supreme Councils in Brazil ; that which we recognize is the most influential body, and is a very able one.

SPAIN.

A communication has been received from a Supreme Council in Spain, which states that, by virtue of authority issued by the Supreme Council for Colon to Ill.·.· Bro.·. MICHEL G. MANFREDI (who was ordered by Ill.·. Bro.·. GRONJA, 33°, with alleged power from the Sovereign Grand Commander of the Supreme Council for the Northern Jurisdiction of the United States), the old Supreme Council had been dissolved and a new Supreme Council formed, with Ill.·. Bro.·. JUAN A PEREZ, as Sov.·. Grand Commander, and Ill.·. Bro.·. LEONARD, as Grand Secretary-General. It is added that the Grand Lodge of Spain and the Symbolic Lodges of its obedience are absolutely independent of the Supreme

Council, and enjoy a complete autonomy, the Supreme Council exercising authority only over the Degrees 4° to 32°, by means of a Lodge of Perfection, a Council of Princes of Jerusalem, a Chapter of Sovereign Princes Rose Croix, and a Grand Consistory S∴ P∴ R∴ S∴. This is a movement in Spain in the right direction, and one that rigidly adhered to will eventually prove beneficial, both to the Symbolic and the Sublime Degrees. EDWARD DE LA GRONJA has been appointed envoy extraordinary and representative at large of the new Council to foreign countries. In the absence of more detailed information, the Committee can make no recommendation to the Supreme Council. At pages 53, 54 and 55 of our transactions of last year, there is printed a letter from the Supreme Council for Colon, describing the confusion in Masonic Government that exists in the Spanish Peninsula, and declaring Brother JUAN A PEREZ, the head of the new Council, a Schismatic Mason ; while at page 57 is a Circular from a Supreme Council in Spain, announcing that Ill∴ Bro∴ GRAVINA, late of the Supreme Council of Colon, had fraternized with and become the head of the said Council. It does not appear from any documents before your Council, or from any information in the possession of your Committee, what was the nature of the authority alleged to be given to Bro∴ MONFREDI by the Supreme Council for Colon, or of that given to Ill∴ Bro∴ GRONJA, by Sovereign Grand Commander DRUMMOND, or whether the action detailed in the letter of Ill∴ Bro∴ PEREZ (see appendix I), has resulted in a union of the discordant elements which have so lately distracted Spanish Freemasonry. It is possible, but it would be highly improper for this Committee to jump at conclusions. They observe that at its recent sitting in Philadelphia the Supreme Council for the Northern Masonic Jurisdiction of the United States took no action in this matter, but continued the Committee to make further enquiry. It is safe to make haste slowly. They, therefore, renew their recommendation of last year, that no action be taken at present.

And here the Committee beg to say that they cannot advise the Council to a wiser course than non-interference where the Masons of a country are themselves divided in allegiance and differing in opinion. The chief basis of recognition abroad should be unanimity at home. When a newly established Supreme Council comes before us asking recognition, from a country where before there was no Supreme Council, it is not difficult to decide as to its regularity, but it is not easy to decide between the claims of two or three rival bodies ; indeed, it is not always possible without personal investigation and a consideration of circumstances of time, place and events that cannot be taken into account at a distance. Too often it happens that the differences which have caused the creation of rival claimants for recognition and for power have their origin in improper ambition, in vanity, in disappointment. Mutual concession, the exercise of tolerance, the practice of one of the great tenets of the Masonic profession, brotherly love, would readily end unseemly strife and vexatious disputation. It should be distinctly understood by Bodies seeking to establish fraternal relations with this Supreme Council that if their jurisdiction is disputed, our action will be very slow.

Since this was written, the Committee have received a Circular from the

Council of which Bro.˙. GRAVINA is Sov.˙. Grand Commander, protesting against the act of the Supreme Council for Switzerland, which, as the Executive Power of the Lausanne Convention, seeks to unite the opposing elements in Spain, and asks the Bro.˙. GRAVINA'S Council to unite with Masons whom he denounces as irregular and schismatic.

ITALY.

From Italy we have received a great many communications, written and printed, including a letter from our representative, Bro.˙. RIBOLI, to the Sovereign Grand Commander. They all deal with the difficulties which have arisen out of the conflict of authority between the Supreme Council at Turin and the Body claiming to be a supreme authority at Rome. In addition to this, the Council at Turin appears to be pressed by the Supreme Council for Switzerland, as the executive power of the Lausanne Convention, to consent to a removal of the Masonic government of the Italian kingdom to Rome. We have recognized, and are in friendly relations with the Supreme Council sitting at Turin. So far as the Supreme Council of Canada is concerned, it knows no other authority over the Ancient and Accepted Scottish Rite in Italy.

FRANCE.

Although on terms of amity with the Supreme Council for France, we have had very little correspondence with it. That Supreme Council has not yet appointed a representative near us, an omission which is probably due to oversight, as we have a representative at that Supreme Council, and the name of an Illustrious Brother was transmitted for appointment. A courteous letter has been received from the Secretary of the Supreme Council (appendix J), suggesting us an exchange of annual publications, and transmitting at the same time copies of the official account of the Festival given under the auspices of the Supreme Council, on 24th October, 1878, to all regular Masons who had been drawn to Paris by the Exposition. It was a musical and literary entertainment, at which 6,000 persons were present, and was followed by a banquet presided over by JULES SIMON. Speeches were made by Ill.˙. Bro.˙. CREMIEUX, Sov.˙. Grand Commander of the French Council ; by Ill.˙. Bro.˙. ARAGO, Grand Orator, and the representative of this Supreme Council, near that of France, by LORD SKELMERSDALE, the Sov.˙. Gd.˙. Commander of the English Council, and by other prominent Masons representing the Supreme Councils of Belgium, Switzerland, and other countries. The music was of the finest character, by artists of world-wide reputation, and the speeches were replete with Masonic sentiment, urging the union and brotherhood of men of all races and conditions.

The Supreme Council has under its authority a great many Symbolic Lodges which are represented and governed by what is called the Grand Lodge Central of France, and which is really a section of the Supreme Council. A serious agitation has lately sprung up among the Lodges for a re-distribution of power, and a re-organization of the governing system, the Lodges claiming that they are overshadowed by the members of the high Degrees in the government and control of their own affairs. Although the Lodge which participated most actively in the movement, and several prominent Brethren, have been suspended, the agitation has not been arrested. The Committee have received the protest, printed in a pamphlet of the Lodge "La Justice," No. 133, and that of several officers of the First Section—representing a Provincial Division under the English system—against the punishment imposed upon them for the course they have taken. This is a matter of internal Government with which we would have neither the right to argue nor the disposition to interfere. But it is worthy of being mentioned as affording another evidence of the difficulties which surround the Government of Lodges of the Symbolic Degrees by Supreme Councils.

ROUMANIA.

The Committee have received a communication from Bucharest, dated 3rd May last (appendix K), setting forth that the Lodges in that country constituted under the auspices of the "different Masonic powers," and after having "regularized their position with the Powers from which they held" were regularly constituted into a Masonic national and independent authority, having for its title distinctive "The Grand Orient of Roumania," Orient of Bucharest, following the Symbolic Rite. It appears, however, that there is a Supreme Council as part of this Grand Orient. THEODORE G. ROSETTI, formerly Minister and Councillor of the Court of Cassation, and a Knight of several eastern orders, is Grand Master Commander, and Supreme Chief of the Order, while the Supreme Council, "the power administrative and dogmatic" of the Orient has a President, Dr. LUDOVIC FIALA, a Grand Orator, a Chief of Secretarial, and fifteen other members of Supreme Council. The laws of the Grand Orient make up a book of two hundred pages, and have evidently been prepared with the idea that a law can be made for every question that may arise. Your Committee do not know what relations the Supreme Council bears to the Grand Orient, or which controls the other; they have no information as to how the new Supreme Council was formed, or who gave its members the Thirty-third Degree, or if they have degrees at all. They are not, therefore, in a position to recommend any action further than an exchange, informally, of publication with its Chief of the Secretarial, Mr. BASILE CONSTANDINESCO LIVIANO, Strada Stelei 16, Bucharest.

THE ARGENTINE REPUBLIC.

We have received a communication (appendix L), from a body professing to be a Supreme Council in the Argentine Republic. So far as your Committee can understand there is no change in the hostile attitude towards each other of the Masonic Powers in that Republic, with none of which can your Committee advise the Supreme Council to enter into fraternal relations.

PERU.

Nothing of importance has been received from the Supreme Council of Peru. Last year your Committee announced that the Supreme Council had demanded the dissolution of the Lausanne Confederation. In May of last year the Peruvian Supreme Council made it a part of its Masonic Creed that Freemasons should not only believe in God, but in a state of future reward and punishment.

ST. DOMINGO.

We have a printed communication, dated 17th September, 1878, from a Supreme Council of this Republic (appendix M). As stated by your Committee last year, there is no reason why there should not be a recognized Supreme Council in St. Domingo. The only difficulty that stands in the way of the recognition of the Supreme Council now asking our recognition is that it occupies territory which originally belonged to the Supreme Council of Colon. As we are on friendly terms with Colon, we, perhaps, ought not to do anything without its consent. The Supreme Council of St. Domingo was formed in 1861 by five members of the 33°, and has ever since exercised authority over the Island, although after about the time of the formation, the Republic passed under the rule of Spain, whose laws forbade Masonic Associations, and for a time the work of the Supreme Council was suspended. It appears to be admitted by all authorities, whose opinion is of value, that if the Supreme Council of Colon would recognize this Supreme Council of the Dominican Republic, the matter would end.

Our Ill.·. Sov.·. Grand Commander has been nominated as the Representative near this Supreme Council of that of St. Domingo. The Committee recommend that the Supreme Council of Colon be notified of this, and if no objection is interposed within six months, reciprocal relations be entered into. We should hear what Colon has to say, if anything, why a Supreme Council existing in an independent country should not be recognized.

CONCLUSION.

In the matters which they have reviewed, the Committee have merely dealt, for the most part, with the relations existing between governing bodies. Their report does not, to any great extent, touch the work that is doing by the subordinates. They may say, however, that everywhere an active spirit prevails, that differences as to forms of Government or modes of proceeding do not check the ardent zeal of the members to spread the great principles of human brotherhood, which is the end and aim of this important Rite of Freemasonry.

JOHN V. ELLIS,
ISAAC H. STEARNS,
ROBT. T. CLINCH.

On motion of Ill.·. Bro.·. MURTON, seconded by Ill.·. Bro.·. MACKAY, the Report was received and laid upon the table for subsequent discussion.

The Secretary General and Treasurer General then read their Annual Reports, which were as follows :—

REPORT OF THE SECRETARY GENERAL.

OFFICE OF THE SECRETARY GENERAL,

HAMILTON, October 8th, 1879.

To the Sov.·. Gr.·. Commander and Members of the Sup.·. Council, 33°.

ILL.·. BRETHREN :—

I have again the pleasure to present the Annual Report of my office.

RECEIPTS.

From Hamilton Chapter Rose Croix, ...	$40 00
" Moore Sovereign Consistory, ...	112 50
" London Chapter Rose Croix, ...	54 00
" Harington " " "	37 00
" Keith, " " "	00 00
" New Brunswick Consistory, ...	19 00
" Hochelaga Chapter Rose Croix, ...	32 00
" Murton Lodge of Perfection, ...	59 25
" Montreal Consistory, ...	10 50
" Hochelaga Lodge of Perfection, ...	31 50
" Toronto Chapter Rose Croix, ...	41 75
" Toronto Lodge of Perfection, ...	41 75
" St. John " "	22 25
" Proceedings and Constitutions, ...	2 50
For Fee for 33°, ...	100 00
	$604 00

all of which has been paid to the Treasurer General. Before closing my short report I have to request the Ill.·. Deputies to see that the returns from the Sub.·. Bodies are sent to me more promptly than has hitherto been the case, so that I may be enabled to fully complete the work of the year before coming to the Council, the rule is to have these returns in immediately after the 1st Sept., but generally they come to hand nearer the 1st October than the former date, and sometimes not till after the session of the Council.

Fraternally submitted,

J. W. MURTON, 33°,
Secretary General.

REPORT OF THE TREASURER GENERAL

Supreme Council, 33°, for the Dominion of Canada in account witht he Treasurer General.

EXPENDITURE.

1878.

Oct. 16, *Times* Printing Company, printing Circulars, . . .	$7 50
" 16, Eastwood & Co., Stationery and Certificates, . .	70 15
Nov. 1, Attendance at Session, '77, ...	10 00
" 1, Do. '78, ...	10 00
" 1, W. H. Hutton, paid out by him for Telegrams re-Simpson,	6 50
" 1, Do. part of expenses incurred by Montreal Consistory, when called to exemplify 31° for Sup∴ Council, ...	22 00
Dec. 20, P. L. Scriven, Wood Cut, &c., for memorial page, .	30 00
1879.	
Feb. 3, Southern S∴ C∴, U. S., ...	285 70
Apr. 1, *Times* Printing Company, printing Proceedings, '78, .	125 67
May 15, Secretary General, Postages and duties, . . .	25 18
Sept. 8, Eastwood & Co., Stationery, Secretary General, . .	30 90
Oct. 4, Secretary General, Postages, &c., ...	10 94
" 4, Wm. Bruce, Engrossing Certificates, &c., . . .	29 85
" 7, Do. Do. Do. . . .	19 80
" 8, Cash, balance in Bank, ...	887 12
	$1,571 31

1878.   RECEIPTS.

Oct. 8, Cash in Bank, ...	$944 86	
1879.		
Apr. 17, Secretary General on account, . .	100 00	
Oct. 8, Do. Do. . . .	504 00	
" 8, Interest to date, ...	22 45	$1,571 31

HAMILTON, 8th Oct., 1879.

H. A. MACKAY, 33°,
                Treasurer General.

Examined and found correct,

D. R. MUNRO, 33°,

I. H. STEARNS, 33°.
For and on behalf of the Audit Committee.

HAMILTON, 8th Oct., 1879.

On motion of Ill∴ Bro∴ HUTTON, seconded by Ill∴ Bro∴ SIMPSON, the above Reports were received and referred to the Committee on Audit and Finance.

The Supreme Council was then called from labor at one o'clock.

The Supreme Council resumed labor at three o'clock.

The following resolution was then moved by Ill∴ Bro∴ HUTTON, seconded by Ill∴ Bro∴ ELLIS, and carried :—

That in view of the large amount of valuable time so cheerfully given by the Ill∴ Secretary General to his office, and the very great assistance he has rendered to this Supreme Council, that the Ill∴ Treasurer General be hereby instructed to place the sum of two hundred dollars to the credit of the Secretary General.

The Sovereign Grand Commander appointed the following Standing Committees for the year :—

On Audit and Finance.

Ill∴ Bro∴ ISAAC HENRY STEARNS.
 "   "   DAVID RANSOM MUNRO.
 "   "   ROBERT THOMSON CLINCH.

On Foreign Correspondence and Relations.

Ill∴ Bro∴ JOHN VALENTINE ELLIS.
 "   "   BENJAMIN LESTER PETERS.
 "   "   WILLIAM BENJAMIN SIMPSON.

On Jurisprudence and Legislation.

Ill∴ Bro∴ WILLIAM HENRY HUTTON.
 "   "   BENJAMIN LESTER PETERS.
 "   "   HUGH ALEXANDER MACKAY.

On Doings of Subordinate Bodies.

Ill∴ Bro∴ HUGH ALEXANDER MACKAY.
 "   "   EUGENE MORTIMER COPELAND.
 "   "   WILLIAM REID.

On Doings of Inspectors General and Special Deputies.

Ill∴ Bro∴ HUGH MURRAY.
 "   "   DAVID RANSOM MUNRO.
 "   "   EUGENE MORTIMER COPELAND.

The Committee on the doings of Inspectors General and Special Deputies reported as follows :—

To the M∴ P∴ S∴ Gr∴ Commander and the Ill∴ Brethren of the Supreme Council 33°, Dominion of Canada.

Your Committee on the doings of Inspectors General and Special Deputies have considered the reports of the Deputies for New Brunswick, Ontario and Quebec, and are exceedingly pleased to report that harmony, goodfellowship, and continued desire for the advancement and prosperity of the Rite seems to pervade all ranks.

The Brethren in New Brunswick are to be congratulated on the completion of the fine new Masonic Hall, in St. John, and the early prospect of the rooms set apart for the working of our Rite being occupied.

With reference to the remarks in the report of the Deputy for Ontario about Manitoba, the matter has already been dealt with by the Committee on the Grand Commander's address.

Your Committee would suggest that the Deputies for Ontario and Quebec, at our next session report on the advisability of a portion of the Eastern part of Ontario being added to the Jurisdiction of Quebec, as they are convinced such partition would result in good.

The Deputies for Prince Edward Island and Nova Scotia have sent in no reports.

Respectfully submitted,

H. A. MACKAY, 33°,

MONTREAL, QUE., 9th Oct., 1879.   *For the Committee.*

On motion of Ill∴ Bro∴ MACKAY, seconded by Ill∴ Bro∴ ELLIS, the Report was received and adopted.

The able and interesting Report of the Committee on Foreign Relations and Correspondence, was then again read, clause by clause, and on motion was adopted.

The Committee on Audit and Finance presented their Report as follows :—

To the Supreme Council, 33°, for the Dominion of Canada.

ILLUSTRIOUS BRETHREN :

The Audit Committee for this Supreme Council have had before them the books and accounts of the Secretary and Treasurer General, and having examined such books and accounts, find them correct, and a balance of eight hundred and eighty-seven dollars and thirty-one cents in the Treasurer General's hands.

The Audit Committee congratulate Supreme Council on the healthy state of the finances, which is largely due to the zealousness of the Secretary and Treasurer.

Respectfully submitted,

W. R. MUNRO, 33°, ⎫
I. H. STEARNS, 33°, ⎬ Audit Committee.

MONTREAL, 9th October, 1879.

On motion of Ill∴ Bro∴ MUNRO, seconded by Ill∴ Bro∴ HUTTON, the Report of the Committee on Audit and Finance, was received and adopted.

It was moved by Ill∴ Bro∴ HUTTON, seconded by Ill∴ Bro∴ SIMPSON, that the Secretary General be and is hereby instructed to print 500 copies of the Proceedings of this Session and distribute the same.—Carried.

The following was then read by the Grand Chancellor :—

I give notice that at the next Annual Meeting of the Supreme Council, I shall move to amend Art. 8 of the Constitution, "time and place" of meeting, so as to enable the Supreme Council to hold Annual Meetings at other places in Canada than Montreal without changing its See from Montreal, and to alter the time of meeting to a date then to be agreed upon by the Supreme Council.

Ill∴ Bro∴ MURTON moved, seconded by Ill∴ Bro∴ ELLIS, that the sincere and hearty thanks of this Supreme Council are justly due and are hereby tendered to the Ill∴ members of the Council and other members of the Rite, resident in the city of Montreal, for the generous hospitality extended to this Council on this and former occasions.—Carried.

On motion, the sum of $10 was ordered to be handed to Bro∴ ———— for his kind attendance at this session.

The labors of the Supreme Council being ended, the box of fraternal assistance was passed, and the Supreme Council closed its Sixth Session in Peace, Love and Harmony at five o'clock p. m.

T. D. HARINGTON, 33°,

Sov∴ Gr∴ Commander, &c.

J. W. MURTON, 33°,
Secretary General.

APPENDIX

CONTAINING

LETTERS AND OTHER DOCUMENTS REFERRED TO IN THE
REPORT OF THE COMMITTEE ON FOREIGN
RELATIONS AND CORRESPONDENCE.

Copy of a letter from Ill.·. Bro.·. A. PIKE to certain Masons in Ontario regarding the legality of the Sup.·. Co.·. of Canada :

OR.·. OF WASHINGTON, April 17th, 1879.

BRETHREN:

It is entirely too late to raise a question of the legitimacy of the Supreme Council of Canada, because to impeach it would be to impeach the legality and question the legal existence of other Councils, which have exercised unquestioned authority from 30 to 50 and more years.

The Latin Constitutions which provide for two Sup.·. Councils for North America, Continent and Islands, and two for South America, were not accepted as the veritable and genuine Constitutions, by our Supreme Council, until 1859 ; at its origin, it received, probably from the Bro.·. COUNT DE GRASSE, the *French* Constitutions, which provided for two Councils for the United States, one for the English Islands, and one for the French Islands of the West Indies, and these *French* Constitutions *only* are still accepted by the Supreme Council for the Northern Jurisdiction.

The Supreme Council at Charleston was created as the Supreme Council of the United States ; and it empowered the Bro.·. DE GRASSE to create a Sup.·. Council for the Windward and Leeward West Indian Islands (which he did do) and made him its Representative near the Council so to be created.

Canada not being provided for by the French Constitutions, never was nor was claimed to be within the Jurisdiction of the Sup.·. Council at Charleston. In those Constitutions, also, no mention is made of South America, in which, instead of *two* Supreme Councils only, there are those of Peru, Brazil, Uraquay, the Argentine Confederation, Chili, Neuva Grenada, and Venezuela.

There are also a Supreme Council of Mexico, and one of Colon, in Cuba, both created by us, and one for Central America in Costa Rica, created by that of Neuva Grenada ; with one for Haiti, and one for the Dominican Republic.

In France, from a day soon after the downfall of the Empire in 1815, there have been until now two Supreme Councils, both recognized by all the rest. Our Supreme Council created that of Ireland ; that of Scotland was created by authority derived from the Supreme Council of France ; and that of England and Wales by that for the Northern Jurisdiction of the United States.

The Supreme Council of Canada was created by that of England and Wales, with the consent of all the other Councils, consulted by it in advance ; I assisted in constituting it, and it has been recognized by all the Supreme Councils in the world, and will no doubt continue to be so.

The disposition in the Grand Constitutions, that there shall or will be two Supreme Councils in North America *(duo erunt Concilia,)* and that as to South America, using the same phrase, differ from those as to the Nations, Kingdoms, States, and Empires of Europe, Asia, and Africa, in regard to which the phrases are ' *unicum Supremum Concilium erit,*' 'unum tantum erit,'—unicum meaning ' one and no more,' only, sole, single'; and tantum, ' only.'

But whether the phrase in each case was or was not restrictive, it is quite evident that it was the present or first creation of Supreme Councils only, that was provided for, and that it was not intended to establish a rule for all time to come.   For it must clearly have been foreseen that political changes would take place, and other circumstances would arise, even in Europe, in the long process of time, that would make it impossible to adhere to the original rule.   Even the great size of a country like Russia would compel its abandonment, and of course it must have been foreseen that the day would come when North and South America would each contain many independent and sovereign states, kingdoms or republics, and when the creation of one Supreme Council for each would become of inexorable necessity for the very existence of the Rite.

Erit and *erunt* are in the future tense, and are restrictive by implication. The phrase literally is 'there will be two Councils' (not two Councils *only*) ' for North America' ; but even if *tantum* had been added, the disposition would still have been necessarily of the nature of those political and territorial arrange- ments, which are intented to control only until it shall be found necessary to change and modify them.   And if we should see fit to create a Supreme Council for the States of the Pacific coast, we should not at all doubt our power to do so, as we have never doubted our power to change for ourselves the Grand Constitu- tions in their dispositions regarding subordinate Bodies of the Rite.

Your propositions would equally destroy the Supreme Councils of Mexico, Colon and Central America, and all but the eldest two of the Supreme Councils of South America, with those of Scotland and of England and Wales, and that of the Grand Orient of France.

The simple solution of the whole is, that the dispositions of the Grand Constitutions were only for the first establishment of Sup.·. Councils, made pro- visions for the then existing States and Nations, and were in no sense intended to provide for all the future.

It is not necessary that I should answer one by one your questions.   The Supreme Council of Canada is unquestionably legitimate and regular, and your allegiance to it cannot be thrown off.

I should not voluntarily have intervened in the unfortunate controversy between yourselves and that Supreme Council, and had not intended to notice it in our Bulletin. But since you have been pleased to invite my opinion, it is clearly my duty to add that its legitimate result is that our Supreme Council, and, I think, all the others in the world, will refuse to permit their Bodies to be visited by any Brethren from Canada who deny the legitimacy of the Supreme Council of Canada, and defy its authority.

But I would far rather appeal to your own good sense, which must tell you that such disputes and quarrels are neither profitable nor seemly among Masons. They invite the sneers and jibes of those who are not of the household of the faith, and win for the contestants no sympathy anywhere. You are all Masons and gentlemen, and you ought to be willing to consent to the initiation of measures that shall lead to complete reconciliation. Invite a free conference, withdraw all contumelious and offensive words rashly used. Remember that you are, above all, Masons, and what vows you have taken upon yourselves of duty and obedience. I am sure that the Brethren of the Supreme Council will meet you half way.

May our Father who is in Heaven have you all and always in His holy keeping.

(Sd.)   ALBERT PIKE, 33°,
Grand Commander.

[APPENDIX B.]

Letter from Ill∴ Bro∴ RAMSDEN, Representative near the Sup∴ Council of Colon, referred to in report of Grand Chancellor :—

BRITISH VICE CONSULATE,

ST. JAGO DE CUBA,

31st December, 1878.

DEAR AND ILL∴ BRO∴

I duly received your letter of 28th September, naming me Representative of your Sup∴ Council near this, and in reply beg to thank your Sup∴ Council for the high honor they have done me, and to assure them that no efforts on my part will be wanting to fulfil the duties entrusted to me to the best of my ability.

In consequence of an indication from our Ill∴ BENJAMIN ODIO an exequatur was granted by our Sup∴ Council, in session of 23rd September, in favor of the Ill∴ Bro∴ WILLIAM REID, 33°, to be our Representative near your Sup∴ Council, and I now enclose said document which I would beg you to hand to him with an expression of our brotherly esteem and gratitude at his having consented to accept the post.

There has been considerable delay in forwarding this, but it was a long time before the Secretary was able to despatch it, owing to a variety of causes.

Wishing you a happy and a prosperous new year,

I am, Dear Sir and Ill.·. Bro.·.

Yours very fraternally,

Ill.·. Bro.·. JOHN V. ELLIS,   F. W. RAMSDEN, 33°.
Gr.·. Chancellor, &c.,
St. John, N. B.

[APPENDIX C.]

Letter from the Supreme Council of Switzerland referred to in the report of the Grand Chancellor :—

SUP.·. COUNCIL OF 33° FOR SWITZERLAND.

28th February, 1879.

To the Sup.·. Council 33°, A.·. & A.·. S.·. R.·. for Canada.

ILL.·. SOV.·. GR.·. COM.·. THRICE ILL.·. BRETHREN :—

We beg, in the first place, to excuse ourselves to you for the delay we have displayed in replying to your letters of 7th August and 4th October, 1878, and now repair it by informing you that we have duly received the diploma which approved our T.·. Ill.·. Bro.·. FRED. RAMUZ, 33°, Prefect at Vevey, as your Representative near our Sup.·. Council, and have the honor to forward you enclosed the diploma which accredits the T.·. Ill.·. Bro.·. WILLIAM HENRY HUTTON, 33°, at Montreal, in the same capacity, near your high Body.

We beg you will remit it to him, and we take advantage of this occasion to assure you of our most fraternal and devoted sentiments.

By order of the Sup.·. Co.·. for Switzerland.

DE LA CRETAZ, 32°,
Asst.·. Sec.·. Gen.·.

[APPENDIX D.]

Letter from Ill.·. Bro.·. CHATTERTON, our Representative near the Sup.·. Co.·. of Ireland, referred to in the report of the Grand Chancellor :—

NEW PARK, BLACKROCK, CO. DUBLIN,

October 14th, 1878.

DEAR AND ILL.˙. BROTHER :—

I beg to acknowledge with thanks your esteemed letter of the 21st September, and the credentials from your Supreme Council, forwarded for me to our Sov.˙. Grand Commander, Ill.˙. Bro ˙. TOWNSHEND.

I beg of you to assure your Supreme Council and its Ill.˙. Grand Commander that I highly appreciate the honor you have done me by accrediting me as your Representative, and my best services as such shall be always at your command. We entertain the warmest feelings of regard for our Ill.˙. Brethren in your Province, bound to us, as you are, by so many and various ties of fraternity. To preserve and draw closer those ties shall ever be my care as your Representative here.

You have, at the head of this paper, my private address, and I shall always be happy to receive your communications.

I am, Ill.˙. Brother,

Fraternally yours,

HEDGES EYRE CHATTERTON.

JOHN V. ELLIS, ESQ.,
　　Grand Chancellor,
　　　St. Johns, N. B.

[APPENDIX E.]

Letter from the Supreme Council of Brazil referred to in the report of the Grand Chancellor :—

GRAND ORIENT UNITED, AND SUP.˙. COUNCIL, 33°, OF BRAZIL.

To the T.˙. Ill.˙. Gr.˙. Chan.˙. of the Sup.˙. Council of Canada.

VERY DEAR AND T.˙. ILL.˙. BROTHER :—

I have received your communication of the 16th August, by which you communicate to us that your S.˙. C.˙. had selected from the triple list, which we have proposed to you, Bro.˙. DR. LUIZ ALVARES DE AZEVED MACEDO, to fulfil the functions of Gr.˙. Rep.˙. of the Sup.˙. Co.˙. for the Dominion of Canada near the United Gr.˙. Or.˙. and Sup.˙. Co.˙. for Brazil.

This Ill.˙. Bro.˙. has presented his diploma to our C.˙. S.˙. and has been received with all the honors due to the position of your Representative.

We have received with pleasure your proposition, and our Sov.˙. Gr.˙. Com.˙.

has nominated the T.·. Ill.·. Bro.·. Isaac Henry Stearns, 33°, as Gr.·. Rep.·., &c , from the United Gr.·. Or.·. and S.·. C.·. for Brazil.

We are happy at being able to send you, herewith, the Diploma of ·T.·. Ill.·. Bro ·. Isaac H. Stearns, in cherishing the hope from this, that that Ill.·. Bro.·. will have the kindness to cement with all his devotedness the fraternal union which ought to reign between the two Powers.

Be kind enough to accept, dear Bro.·., the assurance of our most fraternal feelings and sincere wishes of our Body for the prosperity of the S.·. C.·. of Canada.

DR. A. F. Do AMARAL, 33°,

Gr.·. Sec.·. Gen.·.

[APPENDIX F.]

Circular letter from the Supreme Council of Belgium A.·. & A.·. S.·. R.·.

Sup.·. Co.·. for Belgium and the Territories of its Obedience.

To the Sup.·. Councils and Masonic Authorities of its correspondence and to the Masonic Bodies of its obedience.

Very Dear Brethren :—

The Sup.·. Co.·. has been grievously afflicted. Our Ven.·. Gr.·. Com.·., honorary member of the S.·. C.·. for the Southern Jurisdiction of the United States of America, the very dear Brother B. Jean Baptiste Joseph Renard, 33°, Lieut.-Gen., Aide-de-camp to the King ; former Insp. Gen. of the Civic Guards of the kingdom ; Grand Com. of the Order of Leopold, &c. ; President of the Association for Belgium for affording aid to the soldiers wounded in war ; of·the Royal Society of the Saviours of Belgium, &c. ; died at Brussels, on the 3rd July, 1879, after a long and painful illness.

Born at Tournay in 1804, B. Renard enbraced, in 1830, the cause of the National Revolution. and contributed powerfully to assure our indepen-dence. His remarkable fitness soon called him to the highest military positions. Belgium loses in him a learned man, a true writer, a convincing orator, a citizen animated to his latest day with the most ardent patriotism.

His country recognizing him has granted funeral obsequies worthy of him.

Bro.·. B. Renard was a devoted Mason. We all loved to hear his voice. To a righteous judgment, he joined firmness united with moderation. His heart was open to all generous thoughts—to all ideas of progress which might appear able to be useful to humanity. By his activity and his labors he has restored to the A.·. & A.·. S.·. R.·. the *eclat* of former days. We all preserve for him an affectionate remembrance.

To honor his memory the S∴ C∴ has decided :—

1st—That the advice of his death shall be sent to all the Rep∴ of the S∴ C∴, to give official communication thereof to the Gr∴ Masonic Bodies near which they are accredited.

2nd—That similar advice shall be given to all Masonic Bodies of its obedience, with invitation to commence their labors during three successive meetings with a triple mourning salute.

Receive, thrice Ill.∴ Brethren, the expression of our fraternal sentiments.

By order of the Sup∴ Council,

L. RICHE, 33°,
Sec∴ Gen∴

[APPENDIX G.]

Extracts from a Pamphlet issued by Ill∴ Bro∴ Pike, Sov∴ Gr∴ Commander of Southern Jurisdiction, U. S. A., on the question of the Government of Symbolic Lodges by Supreme Councils, referred to in report of Committee on Foreign Relations.

Letter to the Supreme Council of Mexico.

OR∴ OF WASHINGTON,

1st day of Adar, A∴ M∴ 5638.

4th February, 1878.

To the M∴ P∴ and Ill∴ Bro∴ Alfredo Chavero, 33°, Sov∴ Gr∴ Commander of the Supreme Council of Mexico.

M∴ P∴ ILL∴ AND VERY DEAR BROTHER :

I hear with deep regret of the rebellious disturbances which have occurred in your jurisdiction, where peace, harmony and prosperity seemed to be the fruits of the wise government of your Supreme Council. We believed that, from the diffusion by your efforts of the beautiful and sublime teachings of the Ancient and Accepted Scottish Rite, the greatest benefits would accrue to the Mexican Republic ; and we hoped that no feuds would arise to diminish your good influences and make Masonry powerless, because disunited.

But that which has now occurred among you has again and again occurred elsewhere. The Supreme Council of Peru has had the same ill-fortune. In that of Central America the same differences have arisen. In the jurisdiction of Colon there has been bitter strife between the Supreme Council and the Blue Lodges. In the Argentine Republic all is turmoil and dissension. In Belgium the Supreme Council has found it necessary to consent to the independence of the Blue Lodges.

The same causes will produce the like results. everywhere. The BB∴ who compose the Symbolic Lodges know that in England, Scotland, Ireland, the United States, Germany, Sweden and Denmark, such Lodges are governed by Grand Lodges composed of their delegates. They become restive and discontented under a different form of government, denounce it as an aristocracy and oligarchy, a self-constituted despotism, and at length break out into open revolt. I think that this is absolutely unavoidable. Sooner or later, Masons become discontented with an absolute, self-perpetuating Power, composed of but few persons, and these not bound to render to any one account of their action. A sufficiently long experience proves this.

Also it proves that, when such revolt has occurred, the resort to measures of force does not suppress the revolt, remedy the mischief, or restore harmony. Power must always, at last, yield to opinion.

We have, therefore, in like cases, heretofore advised Supreme Councils in alliance with us to frankly offer the option, to all Symbolic Lodges of their obedience, of continuing so, or of withdrawing from that obedience and creating an independent Symbolic Grand Lodge for the State, Kingdom, Empire or Republic, between which and the Supreme Council relations of amity should exist, each recognizing the Lodges under the other as legitimate, and the members of all entitled to mutual right of visiting.

This is, virtually, what has been done with the happiest results in Hungary, Belgium and Switzerland. In England, Scotland, Ireland, the United States and Canada, the Supreme Councils do not govern Symbolic Lodges, and consequently no dissensions exist. In countries where the Sup∴ Councils have created and governed such Lodges, there will no longer be cause for dissension, if the Lodges are invested with the right to adhere to the Sup∴ Councils, or create Grand Lodges, at their option.

Men are to be governed by wise use of the motives that influence them. Men of intellect and force are more actuated by the desire for dignities and offices, rank, and the possession of power, than by any love of independence for others as well as themselves. If a barrier is raised between them and the highest places, they will never rest until they break it down. When an Order becomes great and its members numerous, there will be many agitators and declaimers against self-constituted Power, as contrary to the genius of Masonry ; and these soon concentrate an opinion which no such Power can long resist.

Therefore, *we* would not, if we could, create and govern Symbolic Lodges. We know that each would soon become a centre of discontent; and that the end would be our own surrender of sovereignty, and their independence.

You have asked my advice, and I give it frankly, hoping that if your Supreme Council follows it, it will find an ample field for its labors in the Degrees above the third, and in governing such Lodges as shall elect to adhere to it.

Extracts from comments of the Grand Commander of the Supreme Council for the Southern Jurisdiction, U. S. A., on letter of Bro∴ VICTORY Y. SAUREZ.

It is undeniable that the government of Symbolic Lodges by Sup∴ Councils has almost everywhere been productive of discontents, schisms, and disasters. When Masons of any Degrees, and Bodies composed of them, become numerous, they will not long submit to be governed by a small body of men not elected by themselves, and whose title to govern is the possession of a higher Degree. Nor will a large Masonic people long consent to be governed by a body of men small in number, who hold their offices for life and fill vacancies in their own number.

Nor, when the Masons of the Scottish Rite become numerous in any country, will it be a thing to be regretted if they compel the Supreme Council to change the Constitutions, abolish the life-tenure, and constitute the governing body of representatives of the Subordinate Bodies elected by them for short terms. Indeed, such a change, at the proper time, would be indispensable to the welfare of the Order.

The change, when it does come, will go further than that. A Body composed of delegates of Bodies of different degrees could not legislate for the various Bodies. A Master Mason cannot lawfully, or properly, or Masonically, have anything at all to do with making laws for, or governing, Bodies, working in Degrees of which he knows nothing, and the consequence of a radical change would be, at last, the creation of separate and independent Powers to administer the Degrees worked by the different bodies.

Invariably, when a Supreme Council has had a hand in making that anomalous and ridiculous organization, a Grand Orient, and has become a fraction of it, it has still insisted on being supreme over the Degrees above the third, and exercising a controlling influence in the Grand Orient. The Symbolic Grand Lodge has always striven to lessen and restrict the powers of the Supreme Council, encroaching upon them contrary to the Constitutions if necessary ; and the end has always been wrangling and dissension.

The whole scheme, in all its varieties and forms and devices, for governing Bodies of different Degrees, sometimes even of different Rites, by a Body composed of Representatives of such Bodies, or by a Grand Orient composed of the several Powers that govern them, is at war with the fundamental principles of Masonry.

A Supreme Council is nothing if not supreme. A Grand Orient is an incongruous monster. A Grand Lodge, subordinate to any other Body, is a Grand Lodge emasculated.

The Grand Constitutions *make no provision for the government of Symbolic Lodges by the Supreme Councils.* When they were enacted there were Grand Lodges everywhere ; and it certainly was not supposed that the Grand Lodges of

Prussia would surrender their powers of government to a Supreme Council.   Until recently we believed that the Supreme Councils had the right to create and govern Symbolic Lodges from the beginning, and that where they did not exercise it, they simply refrained for the sake of harmony ; but being called upon carefully to consider the question, we are of the clear opinion that upon the face of the Grand Constitutions, these give no such power.

[APPENDIX H.]

From the Sup.·. Co.·. of Egypt referred to in the report of the Committee on Foreign Relations :—

CIRCULAR.

VALLEY OF THE NILE, ORIENT OF ALEXANDRIA,

December 12th, 1878.

To the Supreme Council, Etc., Etc.,—

The Supreme Council, 33°, for Egypt and its dependencies, founded and organized under the auspices of the Sup.·. Co.·. of Italy (sitting at Turin), since 1876, and having its headquarters at Alexandria, recognized by various Sup.·. Bodies, amongst which are those of Charleston, Scotland, Ireland, Peru, Mexico, &c., &c., desires to remit the present circular to all the Sup.·. Bodies of the Scottish Rite in order to enter into relations of fraternal intimacy with them, by which means can be established that universal harmony which ought to reign amongst all the powers of the A.·. & A.·. S.·. Rite.

This Sup.·. Body hopes that your power will look upon this proposition favorably and fraternally, and begs that you will forward the name of one of your members, who may be nominated as our Representative near your Sup.·. Body.   Meantime this Sup.·. Council has the honor to submit three names of its members, from which you will elect one to act as your Representative near our Sup.·. Council.

We have the honor to be,

G. A. ZOLA, 33°,

F. F. ODDI, 33°,   *Sov.·. Gr.·. Commander.*
Sec.·. Gen.·.

Names submitted.—RAPHAEL SCAROZZA, 33°, RAPHAEL BORG, 33°, *Grand Treasurer*, Advocate LUIGI, ZAGA, 33°.

[APPENDIX I.]

Letter from the Sov.·. Gr.·. Commander of the Sup.·. Council of Spain referred to in the report of the Committee on Foreign Relations ;—

*The Sup∴ C∴ of S∴ G∴ Ins∴ Gen∴ of the 33rd and last Degree of
the A∴ & A∴ S∴ R∴*

TO THE SUP∴ COUNCIL OF CANADA.

Sov∴ Gr∴ Com∴ T. Douglas Harington :—

We hasten to announce to you a happy event which Spanish Masonry cele-
brates, and which has put a stop to the irregularities from which this country
suffered for a long series of years.

In pursuance of the arrival at Madrid of Ill∴ Bro∴ Edward de la
Granja, 33°, charged by Josiah H. Drummond, Sov∴ Gr∴ Com∴ of the
S∴ C∴ for the Northern Jurisdiction of the U. S. A., to learn the state of
regularity of the Bodies of the A∴ & A∴ S∴ R∴, established in the Peninsula, and
provided with sufficient powers by the said Sov∴ Gr∴ Com∴ in order to put in
course of execution, in case it were necessary, the organization and constitution of
Sup∴ C∴ of S∴ G∴ Ins∴ Gen∴ for the Jurisdiction of Spain. The former
S∴ C∴ of the same G∴ O∴ not believing that its existence was reconciled with the
legal precepts of the Grand Constitution of 1786, and desiring to seek regularity
by the means which mark the Rite, spontaneously dissolved itself, its members
submitting themselves to the legalization granted them by the Ill∴ Bro∴ Michel
G. Manfedy, Gr∴ Ins∴ Gen∴ of the Sup∴ C∴ of Colon, with the assistance of
the aforesaid Ill∴ Bro∴ La Granja, and subsequently the Constitution of a Sup∴
C∴ entirely in accordance with the said Constitutions of 1786, having been
decided on after having fulfilled all the formalities of the Rite, the former of the
said Brethren has consecrated, instituted and constituted seven S∴ G∴ Ins∴
Gen∴, to compose with the consecrator the S∴ C∴ of the S∴ G∴ Ins∴ Gen∴
of the 33rd and last Degree for the Masonic jurisdiction of Spain, which has
been solemnly, duly and legally established, organized and constituted at the
City of Madrid, on the 14th June, of the current year.

In announcing to you such happy intelligence, we offer you our friendly
relations as well as the advantage of a Representative near our respective Sup∴
Councils, not doubting that you will hail with approbation an event which assures
prosperous days to Spanish Masonry.

Before closing, we ought to inform you that the Grand Lodge of Spain and
the Symbolic Lodges under its obedience are absolutely independent of this
Sup∴ Council, and enjoy a complete autonomy, the latter exercising full and
incontestable authority from the 4° to the 32° inclusive, by means of Gr∴ Lodge
of Perfection, Council of Princes of Jerusalem, Chapter of Sov∴ Princes of Rose
Croix and Gr∴ Consistory of S∴ Prs∴ of the Royal Secret.

We notify you also of the nomination of Ill∴ Bro∴ E. de la Granja as
our extraordinary foreign Representative.

We are in the well founded hope that the S∴ C∴ of Sov∴ Gr∴ Ins∴ Gen∴
for the jurisdiction of Spain, legally established, organized and constituted on the
14th June aforesaid, under the patronage and by means of the powers and instructions conferred to this effect by the T∴ P∴ Sov∴ Gr∴ Com∴ of the Sup∴ C∴

at Boston, will merit, on your part, a fraternal welcome, and that you will not hesitate to accord it your recognition which we justly ask of you.

We pray that the Gr. ∴ A. ∴ O. ∴ T. ∴ U. ∴ will aid and enlighten you as we all have need of.

Delivered, signed and sealed, etc.

JUAN A. PEREZ, 33°,

S.∴ G.∴ Com.∴

J. LEONARD, 33°,

Sec.∴ Gen.∴

[APPENDIX J.]

Letter from the Sup. ∴ Council of France :—

Sup. ∴ Council for France and its Dependencies.

TH. ∴ ILL. ∴ BROTHER :

The Grand Chancellor desires me to forward you six copies, which you will receive by express, of the account of the festival offered to the foreign Masons on the 24th October last in the Palace of the Trocadero.

The S. ∴ C. ∴ of France presents to the S. ∴ C. ∴ for the Jurisdiction of Canada five copies on white Holland paper. With regard to the copy on yellow paper, I have the pleasure of directing you to the title of the specimen for Brethren who may desire to acquire similar ones, which are for sale at the office of the Sec. ∴ Gen. ∴ of the S. ∴ C. ∴, 46 Rue de la Victoire, at the price of $1\frac{1}{2}$ francs per single copy or twelve francs per doz.

The Gr. ∴ Chan. ∴ Ill. ∴ Bro. ∴ G. GUIFFREY is at present unwell, otherwise he would have written himself—accept the expression, &c.

LE NÉE,

Secretary of the Supreme Council.

P. S.—In the desire to further extend our friendly relations, we have pleasure in adding to the parcel an "annual," and shall be much obliged if you will send us yours.

[APPENDIX K.]

Circular from the Grand Orient of Roumania referred to in the Report of the Committee on Foreign Relations :—

From the Gr. ∴ O. ∴ of Roumania to all the Gr. ∴ Os. ∴ and Gr. ∴ Lodges of the World.

By virtue of Masonic joint responsibility, the Lodges of Roumania constituted under the auspices of various Masonic Powers, make it their duty to bring to your knowledge that in the interest of unity of action, and after having set right their position with the Powers on whom they are dependent, they have regularly reconstituted themselves under a national and independent Masonic Power, having for distinctive title " The Grand Orient of Roumania " at the Or.·. of Bucharest pursuance of the Symbolic Rite.   The organization of the Gr.·. O.·. of Roumania is concluded by the annexed Constitution.

Confident in your fraternal sentiments, the Gr.·. O.·. of Roumania has no doubt of the sympathetic welcome that you will reserve for the notification of this happy event for Roumanian Masonry, and it relies equally on your generous co-operation and friendly aid to fulfil the noble and difficult mission which devolves upon it.

With the expression of these wishes, dear Brethren, the Gr.·. O.·. of Roumania desires to transmit to you the assurance of its unalterable sentiments of fraternal devotion, &c.

At the Orient of Bucharest, the 3rd day of May, 1879.

THEODORE G. ROSETTI,

Grand Master, Commander,

BASSET,   *Supreme Chief of the Order,*

Grand Secretary.

[APPENDIX L.]

Circular from the Sup.·. Council of the Argentine Republic referred to in the Report of the Committee of Foreign Relations:—

From the S.·. C.·. of the A.·. & A.·. S.·. R.·. for the Argentine Republic to the S.·. C.·. for Canada.

Since the communication we directed to you under date 6th August, 1878, were solemnly installed the definite Directorate, as Executive Power, the Sup.·. C.·. and Gr.·. O.·. as Legislative Power and the Sup.·. C.·. 33°, A.·. & A.·. S.·. R.·.

Having complied in this manner to that established in the Constitution, a copy of which is sent you, the high and sole Public Powers of the Order in the Argentine Republic were instituted, and Masonry reorganized in one grand centre.

The Directorate of the Order is composed of I!l.·. Bros.·. AUGUSTIN P. JUSTO, 33°, Grand Master ; ROBERT CANO, 33°, Dep.·. G.·. M.·. ; DR. MANUEL H. LANGENHLIN, 33°, Grand Chan.·. of the Exchequer ; DR. JUAN F. MONGUILLOT, 33°, Gr.·. Councillor of Foreign Relations ; PETER PIQUERAS, 33°, Gr.·. Councillor of Masonic Institutions ; JOSE FERNANDEY, 33°, Grand Councillor, of Justice ; and Lieut. Col. JOSE NATALIO ROMERO, 33°, Gr.·. Councillor of the Interior.

The Sup.·. C.·. and Gr.·. Or.·. is composed of the Deputies and Representatives of the lodges and bodies of its obedience. The S.·. C.·. 33°, A.·. & A.·. S.·. R.·. has for its officers Ill.·. Bro.·. DR. VICENTO F. LOPEZ, 33°, Gr.·. Com.·. ; DR. JUAN M. LARSEN, 33°, Lieut.·. Com.·. ; DR. THEOPHILUS GARCIA, 33°, Gr.·. Minister of the Holy Empire ; DR. JUAN F. MONGUILLOT, 33°, Gr.·. Sec.·. of the Holy Empire.

To inform you that which remains explained, we write you to draw closer your relations with this S.·. C.·. and Gr.·. Or.·., sole Masonic authority existing in the Argentine Republic, and to nominate reciprocally Plenipotentiaries, &c.

We shall accept with much pleasure three names which you may have the kindness to propose, and we send you others on our part.

Relying that our invitation will be well received, we have sincere wishes for the prosperity of that Power, and we salute you fraternally.

Orient of Buenos Ayres, 31st March, 1879.

                 (Sd.) AUGUSTIN P. JUSTO, 33°,

MANUEL ARECHAVALA, 33°,   *Gr.·. Master of the Order.*
       Sec.·. Gen.·. of the Order.

[APPENDIX M.]

Circular from the Supreme Council of San Domingo :—

The Sup.·. Council, 33°, for the Dominican Republic to the Ill.·. Sov.·. Gr.·. Com.·. of the Sup.·. Council for Canada.

ILLUSTRIOUS BRO.·. :—

The Sup.·. Coun.·. of Sov.·. Gr.·. Ins.·. Gen.·. for the jurisdiction of the Dominican Republic, by its communication of 30th April, 1876, directed to that you so worthily preside over, offering it cordially and sincerely its liveliest sympathies at the time that it proposed the mutual fraternal and friendly recognition of both Grand Centres in accordance with the sacred object of our august institution ; and as notwithstanding the long time elapsed it has not had the honor of receiving any reply to its said communication, and desirous, on the other hand, of extending the circle of its fraternal relations, has resolved to address itself again to the Sup.·. Co.·. with the same object, giving it at the same time a succinct history of its organization, and explaining the reasons that enable it to exist as a Masonic Power.

On the 16th February, 1861, the time at which the Most.·. Res.·. Gr.· Symbolic Lodge, the Sov.·. Gr.·. Chap.·. Rose Croix, and the Sov.·. Gr.·. Consistory, residing in this Orient, regularly executed the functions in this Republic as Centres of National Masonry, five regular Sov.·. Gr.·. Inspectors General, founded, and solemnly and regularly installed the Sup.·. Co.·. for the jurisdiction of the Dominican Republic, unanimously and in accordance with the provisions of the Grand Constitution, sanctioned by His August Majesty Frederic (Charles) 2nd, in the year 1786 ; since which date it has exercised as such Sup∴ Co∴ all the powers inherent in these Corporations of the A∴ & A∴ S∴ R∴ , without which no other Power could have accorded to the Dominican Republic the perfect right which it had, as a free and independent Nation, to form and install a Supreme Council of its own.

The Sup∴ Co∴ of Colon is the only one which,.by means of its Representatives at the Congress at Lausanne, has attempted to dispute the right of this Republic to have a Sup∴ Co∴, pretending that Masonry in this country depends on that Sup∴ Co∴ because it has been constituted, it says, for the Island of Cuba and the West Indies.   However, it forgets—1st. That amongst these Islands that of San Domingo cannot figure, because it is divided into two independent Replubies, that of Hayti since the beginning of the century, and that of Dominica since the year 1844. 2nd. That both are recognized and in relation with all the Nations of the world, whilst the Island of Cuba still remains a Spanish Colony. 3rd. That in the Republic of Hayti, a Supreme Council was founded on the 25th January, 1836, by virtue of the powers and instructions delegated by the S∴ C∴ of France on the 9th October of the previous year, 1835, whilst the Sup∴ Co∴ of Colon was constituted on the 27th November, 1859. 4th. That in order to establish Symbolic Masonry in this part of the Island, in the year 1859 a Grand National Lodge was created and installed with independence of all other foreign authority, which was recognized by many Masonic Powers. 5th. That the Superior Bodies up to the 32° or Consistory degree were installed by order and authority of the S∴ C∴ for the Southern Jurisdiction of the U. S. A., and never of the Sup∴ Co∴ of Colon ; and finally that the said Sup∴ Co∴ has never exercised jurisdiction over Masonry in this country. On the contrary, it entered into fraternal relations with the Grand Dominican Orient, that which composed it up to April, 1876, the Res∴ Gr∴ Symb∴ Lodge, the Sov∴ Gr∴ Chap∴, the Sov∴ Gr∴ Consistory, and the Sup∴ Co∴ 33°, at which time it was this last assumed Supreme authority, as more conformable to the Rite it exercises.

With the object of not allowing the least diminution of its inalienable right, the Sup∴ Co∴ of the Dominican Republic addressed itself to the Grand Congress re-united at Lausanne, by memorial of the 10th August, 1875, presenting it a circumstantial history of Masonry in this country from the beginning of the century to the time that it protested solemnly against all measures that might be taken by that Grand Congress against the rights which, as a free and independent Nation, belonged to it.

If the former reasons did not suffice by themselves alone to give to the Sup∴ Co∴ over which I preside sufficient title to be considered a regular Masonic Power, there would come to its aid the fact of continued possession for more than 18 years, in the full exercise of its authority, without having had to lament the scandal of the least schism, or the bodies depending on it having committed any irregularity, which remain in fraternal relation with the Foreign Gr∴ Orients. And also by ancient practice the Supreme Councils always establish a certain time in which to investigate the original irregularity of a new Masonic Power ; the time elapsed since this Sup∴ Co∴ installed itself is more than sufficient not only to cause this state of investigation respecting the Sup∴ Co∴ of the Dominican Republic to cease, but also to have it recognized as a regular Masonic Power. On that account, all its actions have already acquired, by prescription, a legitimate title to be inscribed on the Grand Roll of the Regular Sup∴ Councils of the world—and prescription, according to the announced opinion of Bro∴ Burke, is the chief of all titles.

The Sup∴ Co∴ of the Dominican Republic trusts that that over which you so worthily preside will comprehend the justice that aids it, and will no longer delay entering into fraternal relations by means of respective Representatives who would make more effective the bonds that ought to unite both Councils.

Accept, Ill∴ Bro∴, the assurance of the fraternal respect with which I salute you.

Orient of San Domingo, 17th September, 1878.

                                        JACINTO DE CASTRO. 33°,
LUCAS GIBBES, 33°,   Sov∴ Gr∴ Com∴.
         Gr∴ Sec∴.

Circular letter from Sov∴ Gr∴ Com∴ of Sup∴ Co∴ of Ireland received by Committee on Foreign Relations, after closing report.

Supreme Council of the Thirty-third Degree for Ireland.

The Commander of the Supreme Council of the Thirty-third Degree for Ireland has to announce to the Council and the Brethren of the Degree in correspondence with it, as also to the several Bodies of its dependence, that on the 1st day of August instant, it pleased Almighty God to call from this life our respected Brother, WILLIAM FETHERSTONHAUGH, 33°, a Member of this our Council.

It is the duty of the Commander, in compliance with the usual custom, to notify formally this event to his Brethren, but he would not be deemed to undertake that duty as a mere formality. The late WILLIAM FETHERSTONHAUGH had been intimately known to him for many years, and it is with sincere regret that the Commander announces thus the loss of an old friend ; a man who has given many proofs of his zeal for the prosperity of the Masonic body ; a gentleman of exemplary character in private life, and entitled to the respect of the whole Masonic community.

As Provincial Grand Master of the Masonic Province of Meath, our late Brother FETHERSTONHAUGH was highly esteemed and beloved by the Brethren under his jurisdiction.   Modest and unassuming, he sought rather to do what he deemed right and useful than to obtain celebrity.   The Masonic bond was to him not a mere name but a reality.   His memory will long be regarded by those who knew him with the same kindly feelings which were the just reward of his conduct while he lived.

He had more than accomplished the usual period alloted for the days of man. He had borne with patience and fortitude the sorrows incident to advanced life, and the trial of long and severe illness ; an example of modest worth and pious resignation.

The Brethren of the Council and the several Bodies of its Dependence will wear the customary badges of mourning for the space of thirty days from the date of this notification.   We also direct that this letter be read aloud in each of the aforesaid Bodies at its meeting next after the receipt thereof.

May our Father in Heaven take you in His holy keeping, and guide you to the end in peace.

Orient of Dublin, 8th August, 1879, V. E.

> J. F. TOWNSHEND, 33°,
> *Commander of the Council.*

Letters between the Supreme Councils of Scotland and the Southern Jurisdiction of the U. S. A., anent the Supreme Council of Egypt.

CHAMBERS, 3 NORTH ST. DAVID STREET,

EDINBURGH, 16th July, 1878.

M∴ P∴ AND DEAR BROTHER,—

I had the honor to receive the deliverance of your Council with reference to the Supreme Council of Egypt, and also a letter on the same subject from the Sovereign Grand Commander of the Supreme Council of Ireland.   I am directed to express to you the entire concurrence of the Supreme Council of Scotland on the views you express.   We hope the result may be that the Supreme Council of Egypt, in consequence of the representations which have been made to it, will declare the Charter and Diplomas issued by it to be cancelled.   As the parties holding these documents will not likely return them, this is all that can be asked, and if it declare them cancelled, whatever effect that might have, I believe this Council would be quite satisfied with such a declaration.

With reference to a suggestion by the Sovereign Grand Commander of Ireland, that an attempt be made to heal the so-called Council of New Zealand, I am directed by the Sovereign Grand Commander to say that he would not be prepared to advise this Council to accede to any such proposal.   Before it could be even entertained it would be necessary that Sister Councils were satisfied that the parties forming the spurious Council were in all respects fitted to establish a legitimate one. But even were this admitted, this Council entertains a very decided opinion that, under the Constitutions of the Order, it is incompetent to create Councils in Colonies. The Colonies are really a part of the parent country ; and if there be a Council there, it would seem irregular to create more. Once let this principle be departed from, and in connection with Great Britain alone, we may suddenly have twenty or thirty Councils added to the roll. If we admit the right of New Zealand to have a Council, then why should not each Province in the Australian Continent, Victoria, Queensland, Sydney, &c., each have one ? Then all the Provinces of India have an equal right. So has each West Indian Island, Malta, Gibraltar, may put in a claim, and perhaps even Cyprus. You will see the importance of the question when viewed in this way.

No doubt it will be said that regularly or irregularly a Council of some sort has been established in New Zealand, and that it is better to legalize it than have a spurious one working. This, however, appears to us a very dangerous argument to use. It is really offering a premium to Members of the Masonic Craft for violating all rules of the Order ; and if it come to be thought that to get a regular Council established it is only necessary to establish an irregular one, the evil resulting from such a course would be great. If no countenance be given to this spurious body in New Zealand, it will soon die a natural death, and this result will be accelerated if the Egyptian Council cancels the Charter. This Council trusts, therefore, you will use your influence with Egypt to bring about so desirable a result.—I have the honor to remain,

M∴ P∴ and Dear Brother,

Yours fraternally,

L. MACKERSY, 33°,

G∴ G∴ Sec∴, H∴ H∴

GR∴ OR∴ OF WASHINGTON,

30th July, 1878.

ILL∴ AND DEAR BRO∴—

I am in receipt of yours of the 16th inst. The Bro∴ Oddi. Sec. . Gen∴, has written to me from Cairo, that the Sup∴ Co∴ of Egypt will frankly admit its error in regard to New Zealand and to making 33ds in Scotland, ascribing it to inexperience and want of information, and will declare that its creation of a Supreme Council in a British Colony, and its creation of 33ds in Scotland, were and are null and void.

I have no doubt that this will be done, and that I shall soon have official information of it. Upon that we will receive the Repr∴ of the Sup∴ Council of Egypt, and appoint a Repr∴ near it.

I think you must have misunderstood my Brother Townshend. I am quite sure that he has no thought of *healing* or consenting to the healing of the so-called Sup.·. C.·. of New Zealand. Bro.·. Oddi expresses to me the hope that, in consideration of the prompt submission of his Council to the opinions of other Councils, one or other of the British Councils will regularize the Sup.·. Co.·. of New Zealand as a Consistory ; which either has a right to do, and to grant it Letters of Constitution.

We all agree entirely with you in regard to making Sup.·. Co.·. for Colonies and Provinces. I do not think that we shall ever consent to the creation of such a Body any where, or acknowledge one, if created.

Canada was in some sense an independent country. But there was another reason added to that, why we were willing to see it have a Sup.·. Council. By the Gr.·. Constitutions (Latin) it is provided that there shall be two Councils for North America, Continents and Islands ; and therefore Canada was not, for the Anc.·. and Acc.·. Rite, a Masonic Dependency of either England, Scotland or Ireland ; and as neither of our Councils claimed jurisdiction there, it could well have a Sup.·. Co.·. of its own.

We shall not consider that a precedent for any other Colony or Province.

I am very glad that Egypt will repudiate its illegal 33ds, whose assaults on your Sup.·. Council deprive them of any claim to favor at your hands, or consideration at ours.—I am,

Very truly and fraternally yours,

ALBERT PIKE, 33°,
Sov.·. Gr.·. Com.·.

ILL.·. BRO.·. LINDSAY MACKERSY, 33°,
    Sec.·. Gen.·., H.·. E.·.

Supplement to the Report of the Committee on Foreign Relations.

FRANCE.

Since the close of the Session of the Supreme Council, information has been received of the death of the Illustrious Lieutenant Grand Commander of the Supreme Council for France, BARON TAYLOR, who died at Paris, on 6th September, and who was distinguished alike for his Masonic zeal, and for his interest in the arts, and in all that tends to elevate and dignify human character.

Information has also been received that nine Lodges of the obedience of the Grand Lodge Central of the Supreme Council of France, headed by Lodge *Justice*, have set up an authority which they call a Symbolic Grand Lodge Independent. They declare that they do not desire to separate themselves from the Scottish

Freemasonry, but only to possess themselves of rights which are accorded to Symbolic Lodges in almost every part of the world. Nevertheless, their act cannot be regarded as anything less than an act of rebellion against legitimate authority. They have put themselves outside the pale of recognition by seeking to secure by rebellion what they should have striven to gain by lawful discussion, and by the action of the Grand Body to which their allegiance is due.

ENGLAND.

Since the close of the sitting of this Supreme Council, the Supreme Council for England, Wales, &c., has informed this Council that, in answer to the application of the Supreme Council of Egypt for a recognition, it will offer no further objection to its recognition on its making formal application to the Supreme Council for Switzerland, the executive Power of the Councils forming the Lausanne Confederation.

The above answer having been received, all obstacles to the recognition of the Supreme Council of Egypt by this Council are now removed.

IRELAND.

Letter from the Sov.·. Gr.·. Commander of the Sup.·. Co.·. for Ireland.

OFFICE OF THE GRAND CHANCELLOR,

30 UPPER FITZWILLIAM STREET,

DUBLIN, 5th December, 1879.

ILL.·. AND DEAR BROTHER,—

On the 17th November last, I informed the Council, at its regular meeting, that the S.·. C.·. for Canada had done me the honor of admitting me to be an Honorary Member of its Body.

The S.·. C.·. for Ireland, having duly congratulated me, requested me to state to the S.·. C.·. for Canada, through you, that the S.·. C.·. for Ireland regards the compliment paid to its Commander by your Council as a mark of good will to the entire Council for Ireland ; and its members gladly avail themselves of this occasion to renew to the S.·. C.·. for Canada the warmest assurances of their friendship and fraternal good will.

Permit me to add the same on my own behalf.

I AM, ILL.·. AND DEAR BRO.·.,

Faithfully and fraternally yours,

J. F. TOWNSHEND,

Sov.·. Gr.·. Com.·.

JOHN W. MURTON, ESQ.,
Hamilton, Canada.

TABLEAU

OF THE

SUPREME + COUNCIL + OF + THE + 33°

FOR THE

DOMINION + OF + CANADA,

GRAND EAST, MONTREAL, PROVINCE OF QUEBEC.

1879-80.

OFFICERS.

T. DOUGLAS HARINGTON, 33°,
> Sov∴ Gr∴ Commander.

ROBERT MARSHALL, 33°,
> Lieut∴ Gr∴ Commander.

JOHN WALTER MURTON, 33°,
> Secretary General.

HUGH ALEXANDER MACKAY, 33°,
> Treasurer General.

JOHN VALENTINE ELLIS, 33°,
> Grand Chancellor.

DAVID RANSOM MUNRO, 33°,
> Grand Master of Ceremonies.

WILLIAM HENRY HUTTON, 33°,
> Grand Marshal.

ISAAC HENRY STEARNS, 33°,
> Grand Standard Bearer.

WILLIAM REID, 33°,
> Grand Captain of the Guard.

MEMBERS.

COL. W. J. B. MACLEOD MOORE, 33°,
Laprairie, Province of Quebec.

EUGENE M. COPELAND, 33°,
Berthier En Haut, Province of Qucbec.

HUGH MURRAY, 33°,
Hamilton, Province of Ontario.

JAMES K. KERR, 33°,
Toronto, Province of Ontario.

JAMES DOMVILLE, 33°,
St. John, Province of New Brunswick.

HUGH WILLIAMS CHISHOLM, 33°,
St. John, Province of New Brunswick.

WILLIAM BENJAMIN SIMPSON, 33°,
Montreal, Province of Quebec.

DEPUTIES.

JOHN WALTER MURTON, 33°,
Hamilton, for Province of Ontario.

WILLIAM HENRY HUTTON, 33°,
Montreal, for Province of Quebec.

ROBERT MARSHALL, 33°,
St. John, for Province of New Brunswick.

BENJAMIN LESTER PETERS, 33°
St. John, for Province of Nova Scotia.

ROBERT THOMSON CLINCH, 33°,
St. John, for Province of Prince Edward Island.

HONORARY MEMBERS.

DR. ROBERT HAMILTON, 33°,
Supreme Council of England, Wales, etc.

HON. ALBERT PIKE, 33°,
Sov∴ Gr∴ Com∴ Sup∴ Co∴ Southern Jurisdiction U.S.A.

HON. JOSIAH H. DRUMMOND, 33°,
Past Sov∴ Gr∴ Com∴ Northern Jurisdiction U. S. A.

JOHN FITZHENRY TOWNSHEND, 33°,
Sov∴ Gr∴ Com∴ Sup∴ Co∴ for Ireland.

REPRESENTATIVES OF THIS SUPREME COUNCIL.

DR. ROBERT ·HAMILTON, 33°,
> *London, England; near the Supreme Council of England,*
> *Wales, etc.*

DR. ALBERT G. MACKEY, 33°,
> *Washington, D. C.; near the Supreme Council of the*
> *Southern Jurisdiction, U. S. A.*

D. BURHAM TRACY, 33°,
> *Detroit, Michigan; near the Supreme Council of the*
> *Northern Jurisdiction, U. S. A.*

LINDSAY MACKERSY, 33°,
> *Edinburgh, Scotland; near the Supreme Council of Scotland.*

RIGHT HON. HEDGES EYRE CHATTERTON, 33°,
> *Dublin, Ireland; near the Supreme Council of Ireland.*

EMANUEL ARAGO, 33°,
> *Paris, France; near the Supreme Council of France.*

EDOUARD CLUYDTS, 33°,
> *Brussels, Belgium; near the Supreme Council of Belgium.*

TIMOTHIE RIBOLI, 33°,
> *Turin, Italy; near the Supreme Council of Italy.*

RICARDO H. HARTLEY, 33°,
> *Lima, Peru; near the Supreme Council of Peru.*

DR. ALEXANDER DAMASCHINO, 33°,
> *Athens, Greece; near the Supreme Council of Greece.*

DR. LOUIS ALVAREZ D'AZEVDO MACEDO, 33°,
> *Rio de Janiero; near the Supreme Council of Brazil.*

FRANCOIS RAMUZ, 33°,
> *Lausanne, Switzerland; near the Supreme Council of*
> *Switzerland.*

F. W. RAMSDEN, 33°,
> *S. Jago De Cuba; near the Supreme Council of Colon.*

REPRESENTATIVES OF FOREIGN SUPREME COUNCILS NEAR THIS SUPREME COUNCIL.

COL. W. J. B. MACLEOD MOORE, 33°,
> *Laprairie, Quebec; of the Sup.·. Councils of England, Wales,*
> *etc., and of Greece.*

JOHN WALTER MURTON, 33°,
> Hamilton, Ontario ; of the Supreme Councils of the Southern
> Jurisdiction, U. S. A., and of Belgium.

HUGH ALEXANDER MACKAY, 33°,
> Hamilton, Ontario ; of the Supreme Council of the Northern
> Jurisdiction, U. S. A.

ROBERT MARSHALL, 33°,
> St. John, New Brunswick ; of the Sup.·. Co.·. of Peru.

JOHN VALENTINE ELLIS, 33°,
> St. John, New Brunswick ; of the Sup.·. Co.·. of Scotland.

JAMES DOMVILLE, 33°,
> St. John, New Brunswick ; of the Sup.·. Co.·. of Ireland.

WM. HENRY HUTTON, 33°,
> Montreal, Quebec ; of the Sup.·. Co.·. of Switzerland.

ISAAC HENRY STEARNS, 33°,
> Montreal, Quebec ; of the Sup.·. Co.·. of Brazil.

WILLIAM REID, 33°,
> Hamilton, Ontario ; of the Sup.·. Co.·. of Colon.

GRAND BODIES IN CORRESPONDENCE WITH THIS SUPREME COUNCIL.

Supreme Council of England, Wales, Etc.
Supreme Council of Southern Jurisdiction, U. S. A.
Supreme Council of Northern Jurisdiction, U. S. A.
Supreme Council of Scotland.
Supreme Council of Ireland.
Supreme Council of France.
Supreme Council of Belgium.
Supreme Council of Italy.
Supreme Council of Peru.
Supreme Council of Colon for the West India Islands.
Supreme Council of Brazil.
Supreme Council of Switzerland.
Supreme Council of Greece.
Supreme Council of New Grenada.
Supreme Council of Mexico.

SUBORDINATE BODIES

—UNDER THE—

⁂JURISDICTION ✠ OF ✠ THIS ✠ SUPREME ✠ COUNCIL⁂

→→1879-80.←←

ONTARIO.

MOORE CONSISTORY, 32°, Hamilton.

J. W. Murton, 33°, Com-in-Chief.   David McLellan, 32°, Gr.·. Sec.·.

HAMILTON CHAPTER ROSE CROIX, 18°, Hamilton.

John M. Gibson, 32°, M.·. W.·. Sov.·.   John H. Land, 18°, Registrar.

MURTON LODGE OF PERFECTION, 14°, Hamilton.

Gavin Stewart, 32°, T.·. P.·. Gr.·. M.·.   Albert Pain, 14°, Secretary.

LONDON CHAPTER ROSE CROIX, 18°, London.

George S. Birrell, 32°, M.·. W.·. Sov.·.   H. A. Baxter, 32°, Registrar.

TORONTO CHAPTER ROSE CROIX, 18°, Toronto.

Richard J. Hovenden, 32°, M.·. W.·. Sov.·.   Elias Talbot Malone, 18°, Registrar.

TORONTO LODGE OF PERFECTION, 14°, Toronto.

Thos. F. Blackwood, 32°, T.·. P.·. Gr.·. M.·.   T. D. Ledyard, 18°, Gr.·. Sec.·.

QUEBEC.

MONTREAL CONSISTORY, 32°, Montreal.

Wm. H. Hutton, 33°, Com-in-Chief.   G. H. Wainwright, 32°, Gr.·. Sec.·.

HOCHELAGA CHAPTER ROSE CROIX, 18°, Montreal.

Albert D. Nelson, 32°, M∴ W∴ Sov∴.   W. Simpson Walker, 32°, Registrar.

HOCHELAGA LODGE OF PERFECTION, 14°, Montreal.

Charles Geo. Geddes, 32°, T∴P∴Gr∴M∴.   W. Simpson Walker, 32°, Gr∴ Sec∴.

NEW BRUNSWICK.

NEW BRUNSWICK CONSISTORY, 32°, St. John.

David R. Munro, 33°, Com-in-Chief.   Wm. J. Logan, 32°, Gr∴ Secretary.

HARINGTON CHAPTER ROSE CROIX, 18°, St. John.

B. Lester Peters, 33°, M∴ W∴ Sov∴.   Wm. J. Logan, 32°, Registrar.

ST. JOHN LODGE OF PERFECTION, 14°, St. John.

John V. Ellis, 33°, T∴ P∴ Gr∴ M∴.   Wm. E. Vroom, 18°, Secretary.

NOVA SCOTIA.

KEITH CHAPTER ROSE CROIX, 18°, Halifax.

Jos. Norman Ritchie, 18°, M∴ W∴ Sov∴.   Geo. T. Smithers, 18°, Registrar.

Printed by BoD™in Norderstedt, Germany